Family Trees and Olive Branches is a must-read for individuals striving to grow a godly legacy in their immediate and extended families. Christina Hergenrader delicately addresses the deep need for families to love radically and extend grace upon grace. She uses heartfelt stories to illustrate both the brokenness of families when grace is scarce and the hope that is possible when grace abounds. *Family Trees and Olive Branches* beautifully lays out what a family culture filled with grace looks like while always relating it back to God's unique design to glorify Him through the family. If you desire to create new life, mend broken relationships, train your children, honor your parents, and bring glory to God through your family, *Family Trees and Olive Branches* is an instrumental book.

Melissa Brignac, Bible study leader

Christina Hergenrader explores families and family relationships in a unique and fascinating way. Her use of real-life examples to back up ideas for how we relate to our families and how we can improve those relationships makes this book a down-to-earth, easy-to-read guide. Short, well-organized chapters help the reader absorb the lessons taught. The author's use of Scripture and thought-provoking questions throughout the book shows the importance of approaching family relationships in a God-led, God-pleasing way. I highly recommend this book!

Helen Genter, educator

Family Trees and Olive Branches is a beautiful, in-depth study of how God works through every family to bring us closer to the center of His will. Families are a gift we sometimes wish we could return, but this book shows us how a culture of grace can bring families into a place of peace, love, and reconciliation.

Rebekah House, counselor for families and children

Family Trees and Olive Branches gives us a biblical lens to see our family. Christina helps us dive into our family tree with the power and the comfort of Jesus Christ and reminds us the Holy Spirit is working in each and every branch and root. Mostly, this book reminds us of God's loving grace and the redemption He has for us and for our families. Because not only is God the author and perfecter of our faith, but He is also the creator of our families.

Melissa Tonn, director of Christian education

It was refreshing to be reminded that God loves us in spite of the issues we might be dealing with in our families. A well-written and easy-to-digest book about GRACE and filled with biblical truths. This could be used for individual or group Bible study. Well thought-out questions throughout that will make you think and also dive into Scripture. *Family Trees and Olive Branches* will give you comfort and encouragement in the midst of your own family struggles.

Alice Rosenhagen, Bible study leader

How do we act when difficult, overbearing, or annoying people wreak havoc on the calm of our life? When these people happen to be members of our own family, responding with grace and kindness can be particularly daunting. In *Family Trees and Olive Branches*, Christina tackles the very complex subject of relational, family drama with respect, wit, and self-deprecation. Using real-life stories, she helps the reader to discern when forgiveness, confrontation, or boundary building is the most Christlike response. Her book is a wonderfully insightful guide to inserting grace into a wide variety of delicate, and sometimes toxic, situations.

Janet Mueller, Christian therapist

Christina Hergenrader boldly shares relevant stories connected to biblical truth, for families to keep building their firm foundation on Jesus' love so grace remains at the heart of the family. As a sister, daughter, mother, teacher, and administrator for over forty years, I think her writing is also a valuable guide for any leader to be successful with the "family" of colleagues they lead. How these colleagues are ministered to with the grace guidance in *Family Trees and Olive Branches* will certainly create a ripple effect of setting waves of grace in motion. This book will be a go-to guide for many years to come in my personal and professional life.

Debbie Baacke, educator

Christina Hergenrader makes two serious commitments in the opening pages of *Family Trees and Olive Branches*. These commitments are so personal for readers, I wondered if she could deliver on them. Initially, she commits to helping readers explore what it means to live in gracious, connected families. As if that is not enough of a challenge, she also promises to provide steps families can take toward experiencing such grace and connectedness. I'm pleased to share that the author met, and even exceeded, these commitments. Skillfully working with the metaphor of trees, she explores the wide range of experiences in families. Once exploration ends, Hergenrader shares very practical thoughts on how to create an environment for a gracious, connected family. I highly recommend *Family Trees and Olive Branches* for anyone who wants a clearer understanding of their family experience or desires their family to more deeply reflect God's design for families.

Kevin Wilson, pastor

The wisdom in *Family Trees and Olive Branches* hits so many places as a family grows. Christina Hergenrader has shared, with warmth and discernment, a vision of healthy family through God's eyes of love. Enjoy!

Barb Tanz, educator

CHRISTINA HERGENRADER

Family TREES & OLIVE BRANCHES

Creating a Culture of Grace in Your Family

CONCORDIA PUBLISHING HOUSE · SAINT LOUIS

This book is for my mother-in-law, Marcilee Hergenrader.

I am honored to raise the next branch in the Hergenrader family tree. You have given so much to your family. Thank you for teaching me how to do the same.

This book is also for Fred Tonn.

Thank you for showing our family—and so many others—what it looks like to live and breathe for Jesus. Your example has changed our family's world. And now, we can change the world for Jesus.

Published 2017 by Concordia Publishing House
3558 S. Jefferson Avenue, St. Louis, MO 63118–3968
1-800-325-3040 · www.cph.org

Manufactured in the United States of America

1 2 3 4 5 6 7 8 9 10   26 25 24 23 22 21 20 19 18 17

If you really want to change the world, go home and love your family.

—Mother Teresa

TABLE OF CONTENTS

Introduction
A culture of grace in your family . . .

For this reason I bow my knees before the Father, from whom every family
in heaven and on earth is named, that according to the riches of His glory He
may grant you to be strengthened with power through His Spirit in your inner
being, so that Christ may dwell in your hearts through faith—that you, being
rooted and grounded in love, may have strength to comprehend with all the
saints what is the breadth and length and height and depth. *Ephesians 3:14–18*

Hi there, daughters, dads, moms, uncles, stepsisters, and grandparents . . .

Summer vacation starts tomorrow for our four kids. They're so excited to
be free of spelling tests that they can hardly breathe. I'm looking forward to all
of us being home together too. We've learned a lot about grace over this past
year, and I'm hopeful this summer will be different from previous summers.
We've become better at forgiving, at connection, and at communicating. Our
family culture has changed from one of frantic busyness to one of grace.

Even if you don't have kids at home, you are a part of a family. And through
the generations, you've created a culture within that family. Your culture might
be one of grace and connection. Or it might be a culture of regret. Or of grudges. Or of apathy.

In the following pages, you'll look closely at your family's culture and how
you can improve it.

My prayer is that this book is an anthem of hope for your family. And,
like Paul writes in Ephesians, I pray that the Spirit will strengthen you so that
Christ may dwell in your heart and that you'll be rooted in love.

May God bless your family for generations to come . . .

Christina

P.S. I would love to see how God is changing your family's culture. Tag pictures
that show a #cultureofgrace on Instagram, Twitter, and Facebook.

Let's share the salt and light of Jesus with a world that needs Him. Love starts with
your own family—and that love always starts with God's grace.

This Book Is Not . . .

Based on Research or Statistics. Sociologists and scientists have studied what works in families for a long time, but this isn't a book about research.

Instead, this is a glimpse into the living rooms of grace-filled families, to understand how these families love one another well. In these chapters, you'll find real stories, God's Word, and questions to help guide you to better share God's love with your family.

A Substitute for Christian Counseling. If you've been the victim of abuse in your family, I am so, so sorry. Families are full of the ugliest sin. Stories of terrible abuse are way too common. Please meet with a trained Christian counselor and with a pastor to help you heal. And then come back and read this book.

Exactly the Way It Happened. Although the stories in this book come from interviews with real men and women, I have changed their names and certain details about their stories. You'll recognize the relationships and takeaways as true, even if some of the unimportant details have been changed.

That's all. Let's get started!

A Culture of . . . What?

My whole life, my mother has been my biggest problem.

I don't know how this is possible, but she's both needy and remote.

She lives across the country from me, but I can always feel her opinion. "That shirt is too tight." "Eating out wastes money." "Crying won't help anything."

To feel really bad about myself, I only have to think about some of what my mom has said to me over the years. Once, she told me that the reason she gets along with my teenage son so well is because they have a "mutual enemy." She meant me!

I have always driven her crazy. She thinks I'm too nervous, that I'm a pushover with my husband, and that I'm too heavy.

If I am any of those things, it's because of her.

—Sarah, 52

Abide in Me, and I in you. As the branch cannot bear fruit by itself, unless it abides in the vine, neither can you, unless you abide in Me. I am the vine; you are the branches. Whoever abides in Me and I in him, he it is that bears much fruit, for apart from Me you can do nothing.

John 15:4–5

The Comforting, Constricting Cocoon of Family

As I interviewed dozens of men and women about family, I rediscovered the truth we all know: your family is your single biggest influence. The parents who raised you and the siblings you called your first friends formed you in both huge and imperceptible ways. They provided your most important nurturing, taught you how to see the world, and set in motion the journey that has led you to where you are sitting right now.

Your first family (your family of origin) is a rich thread spun around you, like invisible gauze that holds together everything about your earthly identity. You always carry this silken armor of family with you. This cocoon traps your deepest secrets, your most hurtful tragedies, and your happiest memories. You could never measure the ways the shell of family both comforts you and constricts you.

As I interviewed friends for this book and heard their stories of family, I could see this gauzy layer over each person's perception. These men and women could trace their current joys, their deepest values, their stubborn prejudices, their humor, and their quirky taste back to what their families had taught them.

Let's call that phenomenon—this special layer on all of us—the *family filter*, and let's look at the power it holds over us.

As you look more closely at your family's filter, you might be surprised at some of your emotions. The viewpoint your family gave you might have been extremely helpful in navigating life—but it also may have crippled you in some ways. Before we go further, write a couple sentences describing how you feel about your family filter. Was it overall healthy? What were some major problems?

_____

_____

_____

_____

Passing down a Better Family Portrait

The biggest reason for any of us to learn lessons for a better culture is so we can pass down a better family portrait to the next generation. Less fighting, more connectedness, more grace.

On the timeline of raising our kids, Mike and I are at the halfway point of us all living together. Catie is twelve and almost a teenager. Sam and Elisabeth, our twins, are nine. And Nate is six. Over the past year, we've learned so much about creating a culture of grace in our house. And yet, we're still learning valuable lessons every day.

Maybe you can recognize our family's struggles from your house too. First, efficiency rules in our household, and to save time, we expect our kids to stay in their prescribed roles (The Sweetheart, The Bossy One, The Scapegoat, The Troublemaker). When we're tired, our boundaries become weak, and we are inconsistent in what we expect of one another. Our default reaction is pride, and we hold onto grudges too long.

Even though our family has a long way to go in developing a culture of grace, we've learned so much. Most of all, we've learned the importance of the family filter we give our kids. Also, we've come to understand our heavenly Father as our ultimate caretaker, the one who nurtures us with love that we can—and should—share with one another. Understanding this has made such a difference in our family.

Here's what I still want to teach my kids before they leave and then start families of their own: you can enjoy one another; your siblings can become your most important allies. Laughing and silliness and curiosity are free and infinite gifts—life together can include lots of all these. Take care of one another with gracious and tenacious generosity. Forgive freely, several times a day. Let your yes be yes and your no be no—but also be flexible enough to care for one another.

This is not only what I want to teach my kids—it's what God wants. Our

Father gives us models of families and the promise of grace in His Means of Grace—the Bible and the Sacraments of Holy Baptism and the Lord's Supper. He also gives our families as important laboratories of first relationships. It's here that we practice how to share His love with one another.

> Next to each of these life areas, write a word or two about your family's filter. Try not to think too much about your answer and don't edit your responses. Write the word that describes your family's attitude toward each of these parts of life.

1. God: _____
2. Love: _____
3. Food: _____
4. Rest: _____
5. Conflict: _____
6. Marriage: _____
7. Work: _____
8. Laughter: _____
9. Friends: _____
10. Exercise: _____
11. Grandparents: _____
12. Church: _____
13. Siblings: _____

14. Travel: _____
15. Authority: _____
16. Nature: _____
17. Sex: _____
18. School: _____
19. Alcohol: _____
20. Politics: _____
21. Holidays: _____
22. Violence: _____
23. Anger: _____
24. Volunteering: _____
25. Forgiveness: _____

Not only that, God gives us the specific gift of our families. These people belong to us in deep and obvious ways. We can see God's love for family throughout the Bible. He blessed Abraham and Sarah with generations of descendants. He created whole nations of His people through messy births and adoptions. He selected certain men and women to be part of the lineage of Jesus. God has given (and still gives) unique tasks to specific families. He still grants specific blessings through families.

Most important: God sent Jesus, the biggest news in the history of the world, through a *family.* Our Creator doesn't clone us or form each of us from dust or send us to earth as orphans—He uses families to nurture us and teach us. Look to history, or to the mirror, or to your own past, or to the Bible, and you will find the same answer: family is God's specific design for and gift to us.

To understand what your family has taught you to believe about the world and about God and about one another, let's see if we can peek behind the filter.

Digging in Your Family's Roots

To understand both the filter of your childhood family—and of the family you're raising now—let's look at the generations before you. Maybe the roots of your family tree are in some rocky soil. Maybe the heritage your parents gave you has been tainted by the generations before them.

Talking with families has made me realize that these old roots have the power to pollute even the newest branches on your family tree. I talked to one family that had been fighting a decade-long war that had driven a wedge between the cousins. In another family, the divisions and hurt feelings between two of the aunts were like a slow-growing sickness. Many members of the families I interviewed didn't know one another anymore. Too many miles and years and hurt feelings had pulled them apart. The newest generation had been orphaned by its oldest members.

Or, possibly, it's none of these, you just don't have the time to work on a better relationship with your siblings or extended family. Sure, it sounds like a good idea. But who has the energy for it?

As you dig a bit in the roots of your family tree, you can probably unearth all of this. And maybe it doesn't even feel like a better family culture matters very much. You have a wonderful spouse, loyal friends, a strong community, and a good job.

But there are three problems with that plan: (1) You are modeling a culture to the next generation. Your kids and grandkids and nieces and nephews are watching how you treat your siblings—and they are learning how to treat theirs. They're noticing how you care for your parents and determining how they will one day care for you. They're learning how to love family by how you handle your most difficult relationships. (2) God has assigned you to your family, both the one you come from and the one you're raising. These are your people. Yes, they are full of problems and sin, and we'll discuss how you can show grace to one another in the midst of that. But because God is an intentional Creator, you can trust that these are most certainly your people. (3) The way you treat your family has a lot to do with how you see God. Do you believe He's your loving Father who takes perfect care of you and shows you constant grace?

Then this is how you can show that love to the people in your family.

Write the major events of your family history here. In broad strokes, describe the family portrait you were handed. Start by thinking of a few words to describe your mom's parents. Then, write a few words to describe your dad's family. Now, think about what your parents taught you by their words and their actions. What did family mean to your grandparents?

_____

_____

_____

_____

_____

Families in Hospital Hallways

God appointed you to the family you have right now. That's a pretty serious assignment. Through birth or through adoption or through a blended family, the people you call family are God's intentional creation. This is the clan you care for and who cares for you.

Perhaps this is most obvious by the moments you share with them in hospital hallways. These corners and corridors are the stages for family drama and intimacy.

Hospital rooms are where far-flung children come together to make decisions about their mom's last breaths. This is where the estranged uncle shows up to get the bad news about grandpa's heart. This is the place of births and sickness and healing and prayer and money struggles and hugs and tears and fights. Hospital hallways might also be where you realize that you, too, are tied to your family _forever._

When one friend had a baby, I sat in the orange plastic chairs in the waiting room with her family. Our little impromptu party included her sister and brother and parents. I knew all of them from the stories my friend had told me, especially about the epic fights she had had with her sister. At Christmas, her sister had called her the worst names, and they hadn't spoken in months.

And then, that same sister hugged my friend on the hospital bed—first tentatively and then harder, and then for a very long time. Her brother awkwardly held the newest generation in their family, and he whispered to his new niece. Seeing the connection of these feuding family members gave me goosebumps. This felt like I was witnessing something sacred.

Next, my friend passed the new baby to her sister. And this new auntie cradled her niece and cooed and cried. Her brother had tears in his eyes too. My friend cried, too, so touched that her brother and sister were there to meet their niece. No discussion about the Christmas fight. No more silent treatment. They were all enchanted to gather around the next generation of their family.

This is the power of family connection. Even deeper than the fights, there's a deep bond that flows between people who share a name, a bloodline, a history.

In that hospital room, my friend shared these deeper things with her siblings. This bond wasn't anything she could have described in a Facebook post about her new baby. This was more profound. This was their ancient connection.

Let's talk about your experience in hospitals—from celebrating new life to gathering around the beds of those taking their last breaths. Think back to those moments and make a list of the parts of these scenes that have been the same. Who is there with you, scrolling through cell phones in the waiting room? Who is talking to the doctor or running out for tacos? Who is crying from relief or joy or sadness or guilt? Write what this tells you about the power of family.

_____

_____

_____

_____

HOLIDAYS: WHEN THE FAMILY FILTERS GLOW BRIGHTEST OF ALL

Today, I had lunch with my friend Kate, and I was surprised to hear her terrible disappointment about her sister and her kids not coming to Easter dinner at their parents' house. Through tears, she listed the reasons that her indifference stung: her family made it a point to gather for holidays; Easter was her son's birthday, her family ALWAYS celebrated birthdays together; her boys hadn't seen their cousins for months. Kate really didn't like that.

Kate and I have known each other for years, but we're not so close that I quite understood why she was this upset.

Then, in the corner of the coffee shop, Kate explained that this particular struggle probed at an old bruise, one that went deep into their family's history. Kate's mom insisted she come to every holiday because that's what her role as the oldest daughter has always been. Kate was not only supposed to show up, she was expected to help plan the whole day—everything from the Easter egg hunt to the chocolate bunny cake for dessert. Her younger sister always got a pass on stuff like this because her parents "have always treated her like the baby."

Holidays, like hospitals, are another place where your family's filter colors your expectations, your hopes, your hurts, and your history. You probably have learned, from an early age, what celebrations mean. They're a time to eat the forbidden foods or to sit in the pew at Christmas Eve services or to get along with people whom you have fought with all year. You have learned your family traditions like you've learned about the Easter bunny and Santa's reindeer and the words to "Silent Night."

You are most likely passing down those same attitudes to the next generation too. Are you teaching them the most important parts? Are you using the time your family gathers to celebrate and also to connect? To love one another well?

Write three memories you have of Christmas or Easter or birthdays. Who gathered together? Who did the work for the gathering? What were the unspoken rules at your family holidays? What did you love most about how your family celebrated holidays? What did you dislike? Is this still how your family celebrates holidays today? Is this how you're celebrating holidays with your own kids? Why or why not?

_____

_____

_____

_____

GOD IS MY _____

Right along with holidays and hospitals, there is a third way that your family filter colors the way you see the world: what do you believe about God?

As I discovered from talking to people, this is the most complicated and powerful lesson their families have taught them.

Your family's lessons about God were probably complex because your parents may have preached one lesson about Him but lived a different one. Your family might have taught that Jesus loves you, but they didn't go to church. Or they might have told you that it was important to be a good person, but they never talked about what good was or the real reasons you should follow the rules. Maybe you cobbled together a fragmented faith with no support. You might have left home to start a family of your own without being totally sure what you (or your parents) believed about God.

Your family filter of faith becomes more confusing when you marry into another filter. If the filter your parents gave you is red, and your spouse's filter is blue, the filter you give your kids is purple. When it comes to teaching your kids about God, you probably find that you're bumping into your spouse's filter on everything from how often you go to church to what the service should look like when you're there.

Again, the remarkable part of this for your family is that the roots of your tree always influence the buds that are developing now. If you grew up ambiguous and confused about who God is, your kids will be also. If you grew up seeing God as a slightly angry egomaniac, you'll pass that view down to your kids.

But if you're clear that God is your heavenly Father, who sent His Son to die for your sins, and whose Spirit sustains your faith . . . your kids will learn that too.

If you're married, write about the purple filter of faith you're passing down to your children. What beliefs about God and faith do you and your spouse share? Where do you not agree completely?

_____

_____

_____

_____

God's Family Trees

Thankfully, God doesn't leave us stranded when it comes to understanding who He is. Throughout the Bible, we learn the sprawling story of our heavenly Father, who loves us so much that He sent His Son to redeem us. God also gives us plenty of pictures of families—lots of ones that messed up, many that showed radical forgiveness, some that failed at reconnecting, and some that supported one another in the most beautiful ways.

So, let's learn what God teaches us about getting along with one another, especially with those we are related to, which are often our most difficult relationships. Sharing God's lessons about how to love one another is the best investment you can make in the next generation. One day, they will find themselves in those hospital room moments or trying to plan Christmas with their siblings. Wouldn't it be a wonderful gift if the people surrounding them are the ones they can laugh with, pray with, and trust? The ones who also understand repentance and forgiveness? The ones who know God as their Father, the one providing the love that connects them?

List your hopes for the future of your family. What do you hope you're teaching the next generation? Picture a family gathering ten years from now, twenty years from now, fifty years from now. Write about that scene: who do you want gathered there, and what's your greatest hope for each of those people?

_____

_____

_____

_____

WHICH CULTURE ARE YOU GROWING?

The truth about families (and about trees, and about family trees particularly) is that the environment where they grow matters. A tree without water withers. One that doesn't get the right nutrients from the soil grows malformed. And a tree that doesn't receive sunshine doesn't sprout new buds. Toxic environments produce sickly trees.

This also happens in families. Perhaps you grew up in a noxious home environment, one that tainted your view of family and of God. Just like a tree, you didn't know this environment was malnourished because it was all you had ever known. It wasn't until later—perhaps not until you began to raise your own kids—that you realized how your family of origin didn't provide an environment for love to thrive.

Your parents might have subtly punished you when you tried for independence. Or your mom and dad taught you that success was so important they equated it with love. Perhaps you've realized that self-righteousness was so thick in the air of your home, you were all choking on it. Or maybe as you've had more experience with relationships, you've understood that what your parents taught you about boundaries wasn't very helpful or safe.

Maybe your parents, in their very best efforts to protect you, convinced you that the world was very scary and should be avoided. This is a culture of fear.

If your parents were especially sensitive to what everyone else thought of your family, it is a culture of image.

If your parents demanded you follow the rules precisely and punished you when you didn't, then a culture of control ruled.

And, finally, if your house was run by an overworked, alcoholic, or mentally unstable parent, you might have grown up in a culture of chaos.

The trouble with all of these cultures—and the specific problem of passing them to the next generation—is that they don't help raise kids who understand their identity as God's children.

These cultures teach kids that love has to be earned, or that love is scarce, or that love is tightly calibrated to performance. If the next generation believes these lies about love, how can they also believe they are loved perfectly by their heavenly Father? How can they share His love with the world?

In a culture of grace, kids see that they are valuable to their family. This truth is crucial for the way they receive love and share love. Because in a culture of grace, kids don't feel like they are accepted only if they follow specific rules for success. They don't feel like they're loved only if they pretend to agree with you. They understand that you love them in spite of what they do—not because of what they do.

Kids raised in a culture of grace understand that others have expectations for their behavior, that they won't always meet those expectations, but they will always be loved because you *belong* to one another.

A culture of grace in your extended family can change the way the branches of your whole family tree connect.

This can take time, for sure. But it is so important because God's love is the message of the Gospel—it is the love that sent Jesus to the cross for us and the love we get to share in our most important relationships.

Think about your extended family. What culture has developed between the branches of your family tree? How did this develop? What do you think it would take to change that culture, all the way down to the deepest roots of your family tree?

SOIL, SUNLIGHT, AND GRACE FOR YOUR FAMILY TREE

A culture of grace is a healthy environment. It's the nutritious soil of God's Word and the radiant sunlight of His love.

Here's what a culture of grace looks like: everyone is held accountable, but no one is expected to be perfect. Forgiveness is everywhere, and everyone is free to be honest. Your kids feel safe because they know they will be loved forever. Family members can be vulnerable and transparent—and accepted for who they are—because nothing will separate them from their family.

Maybe you grew up in a culture of grace, and you are doing your best to copy what your parents did right. Growing up in a family with strong sibling bonds, sweet traditions, radical forgiveness, good communication, and healthy boundaries is a gift. God has shown you the blueprint for the culture you're building now.

Write the name of a family you've known who has lived in a culture of grace. Next to the name (maybe it's your name!) also add a couple sentences about what you saw in their family tree that was grace-filled living. What is one habit you can use in your own family?

THE TWISTING BRANCHES OF YOUR FAMILY TREE

Even if you only know your family history from a few generations back, you probably will have trouble calling it completely healthy or completely sickly. Although you've inherited many of your habits and values from your family, the branches of your family tree are made up of individuals. Over the decades, some branches of your family tree have grown toward the sunlight, while others have withered in the darkness.

Parts of your family might sparkle with love and togetherness. *We have gathered at the same beach house for four generations. My great-grandfather baptized every one of us. No divorces in our whole family history. We all live near one another, and most of us get together at least once a month.*

But other parts of your family might be covered in confusing layers of lies and agendas and secrets. *No one talks to my mom's brother and his side of the family. We weren't allowed to ask about why my grandparents separated. I stopped speaking to my sister after our mom died because she took what was supposed to belong to both of us.*

Not one family I talked to for this book—or that you or I have known—lives in perfect harmony. Even those who understand unconditional love don't always love in the right ways. Even those families who try to show constant grace mess it up more often than they get it right. These families, who try so hard to get forgiveness right, fail at it every day.

Or, sometimes, these grace-filled families endure a sudden tragedy—a lightning strike of pain and chaos—and they have to relearn everything about how to love one another. A car accident. Stillbirth. Jail time. Unplanned pregnancy. Everyone is scared—and scary. Suddenly, the tree is in danger of disease breaking off whole branches. And sometimes in the aftermath, good intentions and Bible-based habits get lost. Even the strongest families have to go back to the beginning, to God's love, and show one another grace.

No family is completely anemic of grace either. Even those that have endured painful breaks, rotted roots, and unhealthy environments can bear new life. This is the miracle of trees. And it's certainly the miracle of family trees.

God never gives up—this is what's so amazing about grace. So even the family tree that looks as dead as a pile of firewood can be teeming with new white blossoms of grace that are just about to burst on the limbs.

Has your family endured the lightning bolt of tragedy? Maybe the sudden death of a beloved member? Perhaps an ugly divorce? A black sheep that shunned the family? How have you seen shoots of grace, of new life, bloom on your family tree?

_____

_____

_____

THE BRANCH OF NEW LIFE

The symbol of an olive branch has meant peace for as far back as ancient Roman and Greek civilizations. Typically, we think of extending the olive branch as a way of ending a war.

The United Nations flag contains an olive branch for this very reason, to proclaim the hope of world peace. The olive branch is also on the Great Seal of the United States to signify this same hope, an end to all of our country's wars. And when Neil Armstrong traveled to the moon, he left a golden olive branch as a symbol of peace to other countries.

Except the olive branch doesn't just mean peace. For Christians, it carries a much more important message. And it's in this message—*specifically in this promise from God*—where we can find hope for our family trees.

Let's look back to Noah and his family in Genesis 7 and 8.

After forty days and nights of rain, stranded on their ark with all of the animals, Noah and his family were desperate. To say that they were scared would be simplifying all that these men and women had survived. (To name a few: building the ark and the ridicule that went with that, gathering the animals, living with one another and all those animals through forty days of rain, and worrying about what would come next.)

Their family must have felt both relieved that they had been right about the flood and terrified about what all this rain meant. Because who wants to be right that God has destroyed the earth and all its inhabitants except them?

And what now? *More* rain? What would life be like now, starting from absolutely nothing? Where to even start? For miles and miles, they could see only water. Was this the new earth? How could they grow anything here? What would they eat?

Noah needed a plan. First, he first sent out a raven to find food (see Genesis 8:6–7), but nothing came from that. Then, Noah "sent forth a dove from him, to see if the waters had subsided from the face of the ground. But the dove found no place to set her foot, and she returned to him to the ark, for the waters were still on the face of the whole earth. So he put out his hand and took her and brought her into the ark with him" (Genesis 8:8–9).

After another seven days, "again he sent forth the dove out of the ark. And the dove came back to him in the evening, and behold, in her mouth was a freshly plucked olive leaf. So Noah knew that the waters had subsided from the earth" (Genesis 8:10–11).

The olive branch was the symbol of new life. Just as God had promised. So much destruction—and now a little green bud, a new start.

As in Baptism, the water had washed away the sin to reveal the new creation God had begun on the Earth. This was a miracle, for sure. And for the family huddled on that boat, the news of the olive branch was the very best. Yes, God had done exactly what He said He would. Yes, the worst was over. Yes, God was giving new life. Yes, it was time to rebuild. All of this from an olive branch.

If you've ever seen an olive branch, then you know it's not very strong. It's light enough for God's most fragile creature—a dove—to carry it in its beak. But this little green shoot meant everything. We know now that this branch meant the world would one day be lush and fruitful enough to support billions of people.

Most important, the olive branch pointed to God's promise, just like the rainbow did (see Genesis 9:14–15). The Creator would resurrect what had been lost. Never again would He flood the earth—in fact, He would save His people through the birth of His Son.

These are the recurring themes in the Bible: Sin destroys, God creates. Sin wears down, God renews. Sin kills, God resurrects. Sin abandons and God nurtures.

Perhaps, through your own family tree, you've seen God's promise play out. Sin tears your family apart, and God gives you olive branches of new life and love.

Sketch an olive branch here. On the small leaves of the branch, write the ways that God has taken care of you. Think of how He provides exactly what you need for your body, your mind, your emotions, and your spirit.

_____

_____

_____

_____

THE MIRACLE OF NEW LIFE

To review, your family is the group that shares your most significant parts. They may have the same face and body type and history and routines and ethnicity and secrets. They may have the same background and filters and preferences and even the same ideas about politics and church and holidays and processed foods.

Or maybe your story of coming together is one of adoption or of a stepfamily. You can see how your heavenly Father wove together the right people and places and events for you to belong in this very family. This is your mom, your dad, your brothers, your sisters, and your grandparents. Your people.

For the rest of your life, you'll see these same faces around birthday cakes and Mother's Day brunches and July Fourth sparklers and as you sing "Joy to the World" together. You are also connected in the deepest ways in what you know about who God is—and what that means for how you live your life.

As you've grown, you've realized that there are parts of your family's culture that you don't want to repeat. Maybe it's your mom's self-righteousness or your dad's anger that you don't want to see in your own kids. Maybe you've even realized that those habits might have a lot to do with the struggles you have with your own family today.

At some point, you've probably realized it's up to you to change this culture for your own kids. That change begins when you stop blaming the rocky soil around your family tree and realize there is hope for your family. Real hope from God, who loves second chances.

This is when you also realize that God can give you the tools to change the culture of your family. He can transform how you forgive and how you live together. These lessons can change the way you see other people too.

It's by design that God gives us our families to love first—and through those lessons, we learn how to love the rest of the world. Learn well, dear friend. These are important instructions.

A culture of grace can teach your kids the most important lessons about who God is and what it means to be loved by Him. Understanding that His love is free and infinite can help your family see that they never need to feel insecure. You can give your family the gift of knowing their value to God—and their value to one another. This is a culture of grace.

To be sure, you will find some struggles along the way. To reverse decades of unhealthy beliefs and hurtful behavior takes boldness and compassion and the Lord. Only He can change hearts. Pray for Him to help you transform the culture of your family.

Through this process, you might also find yourself at odds with those who gave you your identity. This can be tricky water to navigate. How do you make changes when these new habits feel like a betrayal to the clan that raised you? Again, ask the Lord to guide your thoughts, words, and actions. Ask Him to help you be compassionate to your parents as you show the next generation how to love one another in a culture of grace. A better family is waiting.

Most of all, remember that this is the same God who brought out the gorgeous new branch of life after the destruction of the whole Earth.

He can and does create new life, right in your own family.

Write a letter to the roots of your family tree about what you would love to see change in your family. Start this note, "Dear Family . . . "Thank them for what you are grateful they have taught you and describe what hope you have for the next generation.

_____

_____

_____

_____

_____

Sean: An Olive Branch Story of Hope

Our friend Sean makes me laugh every time I see him. Not only is he witty and silly, but he also has the rare gift of true charisma. Sean works as a pharmaceutical salesman and was just named the top producer in the country. This is because he's a hard worker and because his love for life is contagious. Everyone loves to be around our dear friend Sean.

Sean's boys, Henry and Sammy, are our two boys' best friends, so we get a close-up view into their house. It's high-energy for sure (Sean often wakes up the family with plans to visit a water park or to go fishing that day). His wife, Connie, never knows what they're up for on a given Saturday morning.

But we also get to see Sean's priorities. Every day, he aims to share his faith with his sons and to raise them to stay connected to their family. As Sean says, "I want my boys to stay so close that they talk to each other every day. I want them to be a big part of each other's lives forever. I want them to be confident that they're loved by their family."

This isn't the kind of family Sean came from, though. His parents were divorced, and he grew up as a latchkey kid in a home with lots of dysfunction and fights. His mom was bipolar and a raging alcoholic.

When Sean was eight years old, he watched his house burn down from a cigarette that had been left burning. He was moved around several times after that. A few months later, on Easter morning, as he was climbing in the car with his mom, his grandma pulled him out of the car. His mom, who had been drinking, left without him. That day, his mom hit another vehicle and was killed. Sean says, "It was a miracle I wasn't in that car. God had something more for me."

Sean wouldn't discover what else God had for him for several more years. During his years as a rebellious teen, tough years with an unloving stepmom, and dips into drugs and alcohol, Sean struggled to know what God wanted him to do with his life. "My high school years were hard," he says. "There was no one breathing life into me. I felt destined to live on the Island of Misfit Toys. I would definitely change those years if I could. All around me, I saw normal parents who were involved and loving and knew their kids. It was really, really humbling."

It was when Sean married Connie, and when they had Henry and Sammy, that he discovered this is what God had been preparing him for. God wanted Sean to be the transformative generation in his family.

And, now, he is just that. Sean is raising his boys in a radically different culture than the one in which he was raised. Sean is constantly breathing the life of the Holy Spirit into his sons, building them up in the Lord, teaching them about real love by living it with them.

Sean says, "My goal for my boys is that they would have hearts anchored in Jesus and filled with the Spirit. I don't want them always searching for the next thing. I want them to know whose they are. They belong to God."

GOD LOVES FAMILIES

I want to say that I do love my daughter. I pray for her every night and I always call her on her birthday. At Christmas, I mail her sons a little something. Even though we haven't had any kind of real relationship for the past eight years, she is still my daughter and those boys are still my grandsons.

It's her husband who has caused the problems between us. He is very opinionated, and he doesn't like our family. When we would see them—back before this fight—he would argue with us about politics and about our church. We called being around him "walking on eggshells."

Then, around the time our daughter was pregnant with our first grandchild, we all had this big fight. Our son-in-law accused us of not including him in a get-together we had at our house. He wanted to argue about it for days—sending angry texts and blowing it up into something it just wasn't.

Our daughter told us it was too stressful to keep both us and him happy. She has cut us out of her life. I feel so sad that our family ended up like this.

But I'm most guilty about this: I also feel relieved. Life is a lot easier without her husband around.

—Cathy, 62

See what kind of love the Father has given to us, that we should be called children of God; and so we are. The reason why the world does not know us is that it did not know Him. Beloved, we are God's children now, and what we will be has not yet appeared; but we know that when He appears we shall be like Him, because we shall see Him as He is.

1 John 3:1–2

Faux Leather Bumper Pads
(And What a Baby Really Needs)

Our fourth baby, Nate, was due in a couple weeks, and Mike and I were scared. We already had a five-year-old and two-year-old twins. Our little corner of the world was a chaotic cycle of strollers and singing potties and fights over naps and piles of books and getting kids to preschool and complicated car seats and hours at the park.

Most nights, dinner was a twelve-pack of Taco Bell bean burritos. We were barely holding it together. How would a new baby would fit into our exhausted, sweet, busy family? How could we give anything to this baby?

Clearly, the only solution was to get All The Things—everything from the baby aisle at Target, any gadget with five stars from Amazon Prime, a high-tech breast pump, and the Cadillac of baby strollers. I felt hopelessly unprepared for another baby, so I read Baby Must-Have blogs like they were my Bible.

I remember a moment when Mike and I were standing among the faux leather bumper pads in an upscale baby boutique. I squeezed his hand and told him I would buy any of this, anything if it would guarantee us even one night of peace and quiet. (Mike would probably like me to mention here that nothing makes him want to scratch his eyes with pencils like overpriced baby unnecessities.)

It was there, among the baby wipe warmers, that he took my hand and delivered a moment of truth. The new baby needed NONE of this—not really. This little one would need our love, our arms, and our lullabies. And that was it.

Then, Mike told me the plan. Right after the baby was born, we would begin Operation Insulation. We would come home from the hospital and turn off our phones and computers and swaddle ourselves up with love and blankets and hunker down for the baby's first two weeks. We would take off all the pressure and only give our newborn what he really needed: family, lots of off-key singing, milk, and constant snuggling.

And we did just that. Mike took two weeks off of work, and we canceled everything on our calendar. We stayed home and made blanket forts and ate buttered oatmeal and snuggled like it was our job.

This hibernation was *exactly* what we needed, and it's what Nate needed too. I stared into his hazy blue eyes, rocked him for hours, held my ear to his chest, and listened to him breathe. Like a seashell to my ear, I could hear my whole world in his sighs, in the shouts and squeals and voices of my kids. On a gut level—a heart level—I knew that this cocoon of intentional snuggling had been exactly what we were supposed to do.

Think back to a sweet memory about holding the tiniest shoot of your family's tree. Write how this new baby smelled, the texture of the baby's cheeks, and the feeling of kissing a head full of his silky newborn hair (or, perhaps, a smooth bald head). What emotions came with this experience?

_____

_____

_____

_____

THE SCIENCE AND THE SNUGGLING

Ever since, this has become my instruction for pregnant moms: when you come home from the hospital, carve out a little cocoon for your clan. For two weeks, this mini vacation is your vocation. It's your calling to fall in love with your baby in the most organic and simple ways. Let nothing get in your way. You need this, and the baby really needs this, and your husband and your other kids need this.

This is the way I think God designed the snuggling system—a whole lot of nothing—for the first few weeks of your baby's life. Because, from the baby's perspective, all of these people holding and talking and jostling for a chance to bury their noses in his neck is absolutely *everything*. Their warm chests that reverberate with lullabies, their caressing fingers and whispered encouragements feel like soothing strokes of pure love. Warm milk, the kiss of another person, and smiling, cooing faces are radical comfort to this baby. They're the only comfort that will do because this touching means love for these new, needy humans.

Scientists have long been astounded by how important this bonding is to the family and to the baby. They are still discovering the biological bonds that form when you stare into your baby's eyes. This is deep, down stuff. Deep like plate tectonics. Deep emotional ties (in body and spirit) are forming between generations. This is holy work.

This is what family looks like, in the most basic biological and most complex spiritual ways. This nurturing of the next generation is God's intentional gift to you and me and to the babies that come into our families.

And it's way better than wipe warmers.

Try this: Write a short letter to your parents right before you arrived in the world. Think back to who they were then and write to them about how your entrance will change their lives. How will this be a surprise for them? What do you want them to know that this new baby—you—really needs?

_____

_____

_____

_____

YOUR FAMILY ASSIGNMENT FOREVER AND EVER

Consider all the systems God *could* have used to create people. He could have formed each human being from dust. Or He could have allowed us to clone ourselves. He could have established a human-controlled, sterile, and complicated process to continue the human race.

As a Creator, He had infinite options for how He wanted our time on earth to begin and how He wanted us to care for one another. Of all the options, God chose this very intricate design of families, little clans assigned to one another. You share so much with them—specific DNA, all of your first experiences, a bond to one another, and this deep, unconditional love for each other.

Of course, God also uses adoption to form families. As He assigns us to the specific roles of father, mother, sister, brother, son, daughter, grandparent, and aunt or uncle, He appoints us to one another. God gives special authority to these relationships. He created the system of families as the perfect caretaking structure on earth and blesses people through these specific relationships. Over and over and forever and ever, He uses family.

In the Fourth Commandment (the first one with a promise and the first that describes how we should treat one another), God instructs us to continue to honor our parents for the years to come. Good stuff comes from this, He tells us (see Exodus 20:12).

Keep that in mind—God is an intentional Creator; He is sovereign and knows what He's doing—as we dive into the rest of this section. Because some of what we're going to discuss will surely poke at your very oldest and deepest bruises.

Have you ever thought about how God intentionally placed you in your family? Write a few sentences about your birth (or, perhaps, adoption) story here. Which parts of your story are your favorites? Is there any sadness in your birth story?

_____

_____

_____

_____

Dual Citizenship: On Earth and In Heaven

Even though your family is your greatest influence on earth, there is still another family—another adoption—that's so much more important. Your identity as God's child is the role that fuels all the others. Even your role in your family.

Let's talk about identity, on earth and in heaven.

Your identity of earth is complicated to define because it's always evolving and changing. Specifically, let's talk about your identity and the roles you play. Some of these words might describe how you and others see you right now: Mother. Good Employee. Caring. Hard worker. Athletic. Loyal. Friend.

Provider. Funny. Adventurous. Favorite uncle. Healthy. Church member. Responsible. Grandpa. Outgoing. Smart.

The problem is that these identities are constantly threatened, always changing, and never enough. Athletic . . . until you get an injury. Responsible . . . until you can't accomplish your to-do list. Smart . . . until someone wiser shows you how you've been wrong. Mother . . . until your kids go to college. Husband . . . until your wife wants a divorce.

Punch in the stomach. *I thought I was this, but I'm not.*

Who am I then?

The truth of your identity—of who you really are—is that you are a child of God. This is your value and where you can rest. Sin can never threaten this status. Your mistakes, the problems in your family, and the ways your friends have let you down can never take your identity as God's child away from you. Forever and ever, He is the one who takes care of you. You belong to Him.

Paul explains your dual citizenship in Romans 8:16–17, "The Spirit Himself bears witness with our spirit that we are children of God, and if children, then heirs—heirs of God and fellow heirs with Christ, provided we suffer with Him in order that we may also be glorified with Him."

Here on earth and in heaven, through the water and Word of your Holy Baptism, God has adopted you and accepted you, so you have the full benefits of everything that He offers.

This, dear friend, is the best news of your life.

This is who you are and who you always will be.

Write three words for the most important roles you play here on Earth (mother, father, husband, wife, sister, provider, etc.). Next to each role, tell how sin has tarnished or threatened it.

_____

_____

_____

_____

Your Family as It Is NOT in Heaven

As I interviewed families for this book, I heard so many stories about how flesh-and-blood parents and children and siblings had let one another down. I heard how generations couldn't see eye-to-eye.

Men and women, old and young, mourned the relationships they hadn't been able to repair. Parents talked about regrets, children talked about horrific family fights, and cousins and aunts and uncles said it was family members who had hurt them the most.

The story was basically the same: yes, these families were heartbroken and they wanted the new life of olive branches in their family trees—but how? They were frustrated that they couldn't put their families back together after the catastrophic breaks. Parents of young kids worried about their family tree and the young branches they were raising.

But here is the good news: your family on earth is not as it is in heaven. Through your Baptism, you are the daughter or the son of the One who loves you perfectly. And this means that your heavenly Father gives you what you need at the exact perfect time. Most important—He will never, ever leave you. You will spend the rest of eternity with Him. Nothing can separate you from His love.

This unconditional love is the rich nutrient source that equips you to love others. Like a tree planted in the richest, most vitamin-dense dirt in the world, this thick, lush soil of your Father's love is where you find the grace to forgive others. And it's an unlimited supply. This is the power of God through you.

It's from your identity as God's chosen and precious child that you can love your family here on earth. It's because you know that God is the perfect Shepherd, the One who takes constant care of you, that you can care for your flesh-and-blood family. You are the salt and the light to your family because of the Holy Spirit living inside you (see Matthew 5:13–16).

Think about Jesus' words in 1 John 4:20–21, "If anyone says, 'I love God,' and hates his brother, he is a liar; for he who does not love his brother whom he has seen cannot love God whom he has not seen. And this commandment we have from him: whoever loves God must also love his brother." What wisdom do you see in this command? In what ways is this hard?

_____

_____

ALWAYS COMPLETELY NEEDY/ALWAYS LOVING CAREGIVER

Perhaps the best part of our families is that they continue—always—as a constant cycle. This is another part of the genius of God's design for us. We have lots of time to improve our relationships with one another. Decades and generations.

Your family tree is both the fruit and the seed. The needy infant of today becomes the nursing mom of tomorrow, then the doting caregiver to the family's octogenarian, and eventually the wise treasure of the tree. The troubled son grows to maturity and then on to encourage his own struggling boy. The rebellious daughter settles down to become her grandma's nurse and then her mom's chauffeur.

This is the system God established. You only need to pay attention to history, your plans for Thanksgiving, your baby book, and what happened the last time you visited your grandma to realize that family is a unique cycle of caring and being cared for, giving and then getting, neediness and nurturing.

Through our families, God gives us insight into His long view. God uses everyone and everything to teach us about His creativity and power and love.

Believe it or not, the fruit that looks like it will never ripen will actually provide the sweetest pleasure for the whole table. Sometimes, it seems like if there is any lesson we can really learn in life, it's this: I don't know anything because God is constantly teaching me the craziest lessons.

My prayer is that this will be what happens in your family. That God creates new life, a culture of grace, and opportunities to love one another better. In other words, that He provides olive branches in your family tree.

Write a prayer here for your earthly family. What is your hope for your relationship with them? Ask God to provide what you need to improve your relationship with your flesh-and-blood family.

_____

_____

_____

THE TEST CASE: FAMILY IN THE STORY OF JOSEPH

Think back to what happened to families in Genesis. Remember that most of the family stories follow this same trajectory: here's a family God has chosen—aaaaaaand here's a family who messes up in the most graphic ways.

But in the middle of all of these lying, cheating, and killing families, there's Joseph. He seems to understand his identity as a child of God. Yes, his family is a soap opera, but through their story, we get a better of picture of who God is and what He does in families. Hallelujah for Joseph!

Let's look at Joseph's story. He is number eleven of Jacob's twelve sons. Their family is wealthy, blessed with land, has lots of kids—and is a hot mess. Joseph is a son of Rachel (the wife that Jacob loved best), and from the beginning, he's his dad's favorite. The real trouble starts when Joseph, a seventeen-year-old shepherd, tattles to his dad about something evil his brothers have done. And they are furious with him.

Then, Jacob, in a moment of _awesome_ parenting, feels like this would be a fantastic time to weave a special coat for his favorite son. So, naturally, his brothers now want their spoiled brother dead.

To be sure, this same kind of sibling rivalry is happening between my four kids in the kitchen right now. Even without fancy coats and death threats, the biting jealousy is still completely natural to them. Our kids argue over who tripped whom or which one of them gets the last package of Cheddar Sun-Chips. This sibling rivalry is born into them.

Siblings—no matter if they're first generation shepherds or sitting in front of the Wii—always have and always will compete with one another. More on that later. Right now, let's tune in to the horrific story of what's unfolding in Jacob's family.

If you have your Bible handy, look at Genesis 37. What sins do you see already happening here between Joseph and his brothers? Could you find those same sins in your family today?

_____

_____

_____

Brothers, Murders

Back to the sheep fields, where Joseph doesn't have much of a filter when it comes to sharing his dreams. He starts having prophetic visions of himself one day ruling over his brothers. Even worse, he decides his brothers would find this bit of news incredibly interesting.

Joseph: "Hey, guys! I just had this crazy dream! Get this! One day you will all bow down to me!"

Eleven Other Brothers: . . .

Joseph: "Isn't that *crazy?*"

Eleven Other Brothers: "Let's kill him."

The brothers agree that for Joseph's crimes of being (1) their father's favorite, and (2) annoying, they will sell him as a slave and deceive their father into thinking his favorite son had been eaten by wild animals. Eleven brothers agreed to this plan. This is favoritism and cuckoo family politics at its ugliest.

So far, this is a terrible story of family. These are dark, desert days for Jacob and his boys. The favorite son is missing, and the other brothers seem to have his blood on their hands. If the story ended here, it would be (another) story of brothers killing brothers. (We're only one book into the Bible, and this is already a theme. *Sheesh!)*

In the next chapter of Joseph's story, we see what happens so often in families. Joseph is away from his family, and he's found outrageous success. He's killing it in his new career at the powerful Potiphar's house. God has blessed our young shepherd boy with opportunity, charisma, power, and money.

If we stopped the story right here, the brothers would forever see themselves as murderers, Jacob would be a sad old man missing his special son, and the family would realize that selling their annoying little brother into slavery was just a teeny bit extreme.

This is exactly the place of so many families I interviewed: *My family didn't work out. There was so much brokenness. We lost touch with Joseph. I blame my dad for his favoritism. It was a weird blended family situation, so there was a lot of jealousy. We talk once in a while, but it's impossible to connect—too much dysfunction. After I left home, I never looked back.*

But this is why it's so compelling to follow a story to the end. This is why God keeps adding chapters to your family's story. This is why God wants your household to be a culture of grace.

Because here is what we all start to learn after awhile:

Grace comes last.

Wait for the miracle.

God is always revealing more.

Begin with loving actions toward your family and loving feelings follow.

Forgive, forgive, and always forgive.

Families rooted in grace are always about second chances.

Just wait a couple of years, or decades, or generations. God will shake up the snow globe of everything you know. He'll shock you with some big forgiveness and out-of-nowhere plot twists. Buckle your seat belts; there is always way more to come.

> What twist in your family is still unresolved? Maybe it has been a divorce, a terrible illness, or a family feud. Write your prayer of what olive branch you hope God will give your family.
>
> _____
>
> _____
>
> _____
>
> _____

SUCCESSES! FAILURES! STILL NOT THE END OF THE STORY!

Then, Genesis 39 happens, and here is the stuff of blockbuster movies. We see Joseph off in the Washington DC of Egypt, living as a top aide to Potiphar. Joseph has the smarts and political charisma of JFK and is loved by all. Unfortunately, Joseph is really loved by Potiphar's wife. She is corrupt and invents a story about Joseph attacking her. All of this turns out to be really bad news for our hero, Joseph. His story (once again) feels over.

It's at about this point in the story that Joseph starts to look a lot like my dear friend Tanya's strange son. His name is Daniel, and he lives in a tiny apartment with only a kitchen, a toilet, and a mattress—in the very worst part of Houston. He is unemployed, doesn't have a car, and struggles with dark mental illness. We all worry about him constantly, so afraid his parents will get the call that he's been hurt—or hurt himself.

We try to help too. We pray for him, and we set up job interviews and counseling appointments for him. But he is bitter and odd, and these never work out well. Last year, my husband had arranged for Daniel to work with a friend who was starting a window-cleaning business.

But then Daniel called the entrepreneur and delivered a long, rambling argument about how he doesn't think the business will work because people only get their windows cleaned in the summer. As a conclusion, he told the window-cleaning guy, "You won't have enough revenue for the winter. You'll go out of business."

At this point, the window washer hung up and was angry for months about the conversation. Tanya and her husband were so embarrassed. Their friends circled around them to listen and speculate about why Daniel does peculiar, difficult things like this.

But then it turned out that people only want their windows cleaned in the summer. The guy starting the business hadn't planned for that, and his new company had to declare bankruptcy. We were all sad for him, but I couldn't stop thinking: this was the warning that Daniel had given him months ago.

I had lunch with Tanya that week and she said, "My son is hard and difficult. But sometimes, it feels like he's a kind of a prophet. He tells the truth that no one wants to hear. And he's usually right. Even if no one likes him very much."

Joseph was probably a little like this with his dreams. Even in prison, where it's very wise to make friends with the other guys who share your bed and toilet, Joseph told the truth. This seemed like just an awful idea, as it made some of them very mad. But this was Joseph—always minutes from someone murdering him, and he kept telling the truth.

And, hey! What do you know? Telling the truth actually worked out really well for Joseph. Even if Joseph had temporarily lost his family, he still belonged to God. And God was taking care of him with these unique dreams.

Pharaoh, the ruler of the most powerful country, asked Joseph to work for him as his right-hand man. Pharaoh hiring Joseph would be like the CEO of ExxonMobil calling our friend Daniel and asking him to help him forecast the price of oil over the next decade.

Joseph predicts seven years of bumper crops in Egypt followed by seven years of severe famine. He advises the king to begin storing grain to prepare for the coming famine. For his wisdom, Joseph is made a ruler in Egypt, second only to the king.

Again, for anyone following this story, it would seem like Joseph just won. If this were the end of the book, it would be an epic tale about how our hero overcame his broken, weird family situation to rise to power and help his country.

Roll the credits, close the novel, the message here is, "You, too, can leave behind the toxic soil of your family tree to make something of yourself!"

Rock on, Joseph. Write your celebrity memoir—it will sell millions of copies.

Except . . . God isn't even close to finished with Joseph's story.

This is a familiar tale: the promising son leaves his dysfunctional home to make it big in the world. What happens in these stories in books and movies? Can you ever really leave your family behind? Why or why not?

_____

_____

_____

_____

The Picture of Success?

Joseph has truly arrived at success. Pharaoh loves him and cannot find enough ways to bless and praise and create a cushy life for Joseph. Here, we see

Joseph's old charisma: the stuff that made Jacob weave him a special coat, and his brothers hate him, and Potiphar see something special in him—Potiphar's wife *really* see something special in him—and now Pharaoh is celebrating him as the darling of the rich and powerful set.

But back on the farm, there's a famine and Jacob's clan is starving. If his story were on the Biography channel, there would be footage of Joseph's poor, misguided family huddled together with hungry scowls on their faces. Then, the scene would quickly cut to Joseph wearing Pharaoh's signet ring, dressed in the finest clothes imaginable, kissing his new wife. End of the story, right?

The clear moral of this story would be that not even messed-up parents can dampen true charisma! When even the pharaoh sees that God has chosen you, it's for real. Look at Joseph now! He's unrecognizable as a powerful millionaire. No one from the old clan would even know it was the same shepherd kid. He's got the nice clothes, the eye-bulging jewelry, the high-society wife. In short: Joseph is now the portrait of a kid from the wrong side of the tracks who has made it big.

In extended families, we love to characterize whole sides of the family as "the rich side" or "the ones who have trouble with money" or "the part of the family that doesn't go to church." What do you think other parts of your family would call your branch of the family tree? Is this accurate?

_____

_____

_____

_____

THE WELFARE RELATIONS COME BEGGING

Meanwhile, back at home, the poor relations are still struggling. In a desperate attempt to survive, Jacob sends his boys to Egypt to get some food for their people. The ten other sons (Benjamin, the youngest, stays home with their dad) leave the ghetto that their hometown has become to travel to the big city and apply for the ancient version of food stamps.

But just like anyone trying to get government aid, they find the process isn't simple. Not far into their welfare plea, the ten brothers find themselves bowed down at Joseph's feet. They must be dealing with some serious hyperglycemia because they don't recognize Joseph as their long-lost little brother.

OF COURSE Joseph remembers this scene from the movie playing in his mind because he is the kind of exceptional, odd bird who always knew this would happen. Maybe no one could have guessed the weird, twisted details, but Joseph recalls this all the way back from when he was just that annoying little brother in the cool coat. This is what he dreamed would happen.

Finally, we're at the great climax. Now the story will end with Joseph's chance to take vengeance on his brothers. Here is the scene where he punishes his mean, selfish, murdering family. The moral of the story will be that the bad people TOTALLY got what they deserve.

HA! Take that, brothers who threw me in the well. You sold me into slavery, but now you're the slaves and I'm your master.

The clear villains here are Jacob's sons. The Death Star is now exploding, and naming your kids after one of Joseph's brothers would be like calling him Darth Vader. These guys are the bad seeds and God hates them.

Right?

Someone in your family is the bad seed, right? But wait. Are they really? In making this person a villain, have you given them superhuman abilities to hurt you and mess up your family? Is this person really that powerful? Have you ever discovered that this person's reputation doesn't really fit them at all? Write that story here.

_____

_____

_____

_____

WAIT. WHAT? JOSEPH REALLY IS CRAZY!

Except none of that happens at all. Here, Joseph changes the story AGAIN and tells his brothers: "Go bring back Benjamin, your youngest brother; then I'll know you're not spies. Then I'll give you grain." What is Joseph doing? How is he going to throw them into prison and take his revenge if he's letting them go back *home*?

The brothers scramble to do the right thing and hurry back to Egypt with Benjamin. More than anything, they want to do whatever this benevolent Egyptian ruler tells them to, so they can get food in their bellies.

Perhaps this is where the lens twists just a bit so we can see that this is also the story of the brothers. God doesn't leave the bad seeds alone to rot without His help. They still belong to Him, they are still His children, and He is still caring for each and every one of them.

This is where we remember that life isn't the movies, and no one is ever completely the hero or villain. God loves each and every one of us. He redeemed Joseph when He pulled him out of the well. Then, He pulled him out of prison. This is where God takes care of the brothers with a second chance. Grain for all! And straight from their least likely benefactor.

Wouldn't this be an unpopular twist in a movie? The reviews would be scathing: *One star! No redeemable qualities in the characters and totally unbelievable plot twists! I hated this story!*

Yet, when God tells a story, we learn the better message for all of us. Our Father is all about second (third, fourth, infinite) chances for everyone. "Forgiveness for you! Forgiveness for you! And you! And you! New life for everyone! Olive branches everywhere!"

The rest of the story is that this back-stabbing, sinful, despicable, unlovable family ends up together. Jacob's descendants stay in Egypt for four hundred years, until the time of Moses. And when Moses leads the Hebrews out of Egypt, he carries Joseph's bones on his back.

Now THAT is a legacy.

What headline fits your own family's story? Disaster Tears Family Apart or Forgiveness Reunites Everyone or Happy Family Realizes Their Life Is a Lie or Years of Alcoholism Rips Family. Write some of the headlines here that describe your family.

_____

_____

_____

_____

THE POINT OF THE STORY

You could tell your family's story and it would probably have similar twists to Joseph's. Family trees are not only filled with olive branches, but they're also poisoned with noxious nuts, sickly thorns, and lots of bad fruit. Surely, if we had stopped Joseph's story at any of the critical spots, it would have had a different point. The lesson would have been that family is temporary. Grace can't grow in such a toxic environment. Some parts of your family aren't worthy of forgiveness.

But God turns all that around and shows us that the story was about grace the whole time. He keeps the tree growing. As the rings expand further and further, we see the brighter picture that's developing. He blesses the family with the flexibility to forgive one another. He gives them their original family portrait back—yes, it's filled with some deep scars, but the family remains intact.

Clearly, the story God is telling here is that He takes care of every single one of His children, and that it's never too late for a second chance, and the story isn't over until He, the Lord, says it's over.

Perhaps most profoundly, Joseph's story presents amazing insight into how God works to overcome evil and bring about His plan. After all his tragedies, Joseph still understands that he belongs to God. That's his most important identity. Yes, he's been assigned this messed-up bunch of brothers here on Earth, but this isn't where his true value is.

At the end of Joseph's story, he tells his brothers who he is. He talks about their sin this way: "Do not be distressed or angry with yourselves because you sold me here, for God sent me before you to preserve life. . . . So it was not you who sent me here, but God" (Genesis 45:5, 8). Later, Joseph again reassures his brothers, offering forgiveness and saying, "You meant evil against me, but God meant it for good" (Genesis 50:20).

Oh, YES to Genesis 50:20. I feel like I need to tattoo that on my forehead—and on the foreheads of everyone I know. Because we ALWAYS see the evil brought against us. We ALWAYS feel so confident that we have come to the end of the story. Conventional wisdom tells us: "Walk away from your toxic family tree because it's not worth watering." Or, "Your family's story is over and dead and ended with the truth that you are a victim." Or, "You are the star of the universe and don't let anyone get in your way. Your family is not worth your time." Or, "Building a culture of grace in your family is going to be impossible. Look at the messed-up people you come from. Give up now. Don't even try for the next generation. They're doomed too. People are just too selfish."

Joseph shows us a different ending, though, and it's certainly the better one. The story of Joseph encourages us to take the less self-centered view of family and teaches us the lesson that God is always the Author of our stories. And He doesn't have heroes or villains or simple endings. God has grace. Always grace. The kind of grace we can build into our families' cultures right now.

Give an example of bad advice the world has given you about your family and forgiveness. How was this a faulty view?

_____

_____

_____

_____

BETTER THAN THAT SIGNET RING

If you've ever had a moment of spiritual clarity like Joseph does in Genesis 50:20, you know the deep comfort it brings. These moments of understanding what God was up to all the time feel like a wink from Him.

You trust in God's sovereignty and radical care for you. It feels like forgiveness and love are totally possible because they are your Father's greatest blessings. Olive branches are just about to burst through on the deadest and most difficult branches of your family tree. With God, you will forgive. You will be the salt and light.

You know what this all kind of feels like? Time travel. By understanding that God works across seasons and through hard lessons, Joseph can say to himself, "Wait. Rewind back to when my brothers wanted to kill me. Now fast forward to that moment I forgave them and we hugged it out. Who would have thought? But that was all totally You, God."

In the same way, you and I can see how God builds a culture of grace in our homes through seasons, through twists and turns, through slow-growing olive branches. With this view of your family, you can see that the culture of grace you are praying for is coming gradually, through the perfect care of your Father.

Through this, you can say, "Lord, remember that moment when I was convinced that my sisters would never forgive me for throwing away Mom's peanut brittle recipe? Or, remember when we thought we had lost our son, when we thought repentance and forgiveness were impossible? And, rewind back to when our daughter yelled every morning at breakfast and we wanted to trade her in for an easier relationship. But look! We didn't even know the surprises you had in store for us, Father. We never could have seen the grace that was glittering all over those seasons. But now we do."

As we talk about growing olive branches in your family tree, we'll discuss how sin will often spew its herbicide all over the culture of grace in your family tree. Pride, perhaps the very worst chainsaw to olive branches, can slice off entire generations. Poor boundaries and families who get stuck in their roles also have a deadly effect on fragile shoots of grace. But there is hope—always hope.

Joseph's family was like the picture of all of these bad family habits. And yet, God still cared for them. Their story didn't end in sin and separation. Joseph's family story ends in a celebration with millions of fragrant olive branches blooming all over his sprawling, beautiful tree.

Tell a time travel story of your family. When have you found yourself marveling at how God has cared for your people? When has He helped you forgive one another? Tell that story here.

_____

_____

_____

_____

YOUR STORY ISN'T OVER

The beautiful, crazy part of trees—and much more important, FAMILY trees—is that they keep sprouting new parts. Trees are regenerative, which means those fresh blooms come year after year. God gives your family new life and forgiveness too. To feel like you know that your family's story ends badly is about as premature as cutting down an apple tree in January because it looks dead.

That tree looks as alive to God when it's covered in snow as it will to you in June. He sees the buds that will burst forth. He knows about spring and the new leaves that will be so green and brilliant they will look photoshopped. He can already count the apples you will collect from this tree and the pies you will make from them and how many jars of applesauce you can store.

So when you pull out your chainsaw, God is (obviously) shaking His head. Again, we ALWAYS write people off way too soon. We have black belts in quick, shallow judgment. We have PhDs in short-sightedness and paranoia. We never understand the full story.

God specializes in the long view, radical and ridiculous grace for all, and He teaches us to trust and gives us faith so we can. He is mystical, outrageous love that spans generations. He cares for us as we walk through the valley of the shadow of death. We don't have to fear evil because His staff and rod comfort us (Psalm 23:4). In other words, He has plans for your family that will turn everything you know right on its head.

YOU are some long ago relative's dream come true. Reading this book and praying for the ancient tree of your family is what your grandmother or great aunts hoped for.

And maybe the next generation will find this book and love that you took the time to write notes about your family on its pages. God already knows what lessons your descendants will need. He will take perfect care of them too.

That's the promise of olive branches.

Look at Psalm 23:4. These words have comforted so many generations of God's people. Think about God's promise to take care of you, and relate that to your family right now. What kind of care do you need today?

_____

_____

_____

_____

LET'S CELEBRATE
DAS GLÜCKLICHE FEST DER SOUVERÄNITÄT GOTTES!

I wish we had a holiday to celebrate Joseph's words in Genesis 50:20: "As for you, you meant evil against me, but God meant it for good, to bring it about that many people should be kept alive, as they are today."

Maybe to help us all remember that God knows the bigger picture and cares for us through our doubts, we should hold a three-day festival to remind one another about Joseph's spiritual truth at the end of his story. This would help us celebrate the new life—the olive branches—that God is always growing in our family trees.

We could gather with our extended family and commemorate the idea that we have dual citizenship—as belonging to God but also belonging to one another. We care for one another because God cares for us. We are capable of love because of God's love for us. We forgive because He forgave us. The culture of grace in our families will be the salt and the light to the world.

We need some kind of an observance to help us remember all this. For this celebration, we could do all kinds of practices to commemorate the fact that we can understand our stories of belonging to one another best when we understand that our gracious God is the Author of them. He is the one providing the nutrients our family trees need.

On the first day of our special festival, we would meet in a home with lots of wonderful cakes and favorite hymns. Maybe as a nice touch, we could all wear brightly colored coats, like Joseph's. And, oh! We could gather around a large table and write down everything that had gone wrong in our family that year. We could write it all on pretty papers with very nice pens. Maybe that would make it easier to scribble down the really painful parts.

Then, on the second day, we would say things to one another like, "Dear brother, you hurt our feelings when you blew off the annual Memorial Day barbecue. But it's OKAY! We understand that your new wife doesn't like fried chicken and thinks that our venison sausage is disgusting, and you were caught between us and her loyalty to PETA. That's a tough situation you were in, brother."

We would then hold hands with him and say, "But we are your family and we love you and forgive you all the time. Even though your wife probably wants us all to go away, we are learning how to love her. We are trusting God that something better is coming! We want grace to rule in this family, and that starts right here with telling you how much we love you."

Maybe we could look him in the eye and say kind words like, "Through this, God is teaching us how to forgive, and through that, we're also learning how to repent and accept being forgiven. So yes, with the help of the Holy Spirit, we are even learning how to tolerate her vegan rants. All this to say, we are better at understanding God's love through this because He is so good at taking care of each and every one of us!

"Even though God probably also thinks that your new wife could just eat the cheeseburger."

(Okay, we wouldn't say the last part. But because we are sinful, we would probably think it.)

Then, on the third day of the festival, we would burn all of the grievances. Or maybe we would bury them because it's such a nice metaphor for family trees. Anyway, we would have some kind of a quaint ceremony involving lots of pie and confetti and sparklers and a gift exchange. Because pie and sparklers and gifts make everything feel festive.

Then, finally, we would all take turns marveling at how we temporarily got caught up in our own short-sighted paranoia, but how God is always doing something so much better for us all. I think we would call this the Joseph Festival. Or The Celebration of Second Chances.

Or better yet, let's give it some complicated German name that means, "All of us are very messed up, and because of that, we don't know anything about how to love or forgive or take care of one another, but God does, so let's eat pie and try to remember that during the next year!"

I think this sounds fantastic.

Who's in?

What about you? What do you love about Joseph's lesson in Genesis 50:20? What would change if you could understand God's sovereignty better? Could you trust Him more? How? What's your prayer for this in your family?

Anna: An Olive Branch Story of Hope

Our dear friend, Anna, is our twins' adorable, bubbly third-grade teacher, and she also attends our church. The kids in her class love her, and they follow her like she's leaving behind a trail of M&M's. She teaches our kids everything from quadrilaterals to cursive and also answers their deep theological questions. We all love Anna. We couldn't wait for her to become a mom. Anna couldn't wait either.

But fertility and pregnancy had been struggles for Anna and her husband, John. They had been married for five years and still hadn't been able to have kids. After several miscarriages, they decided to adopt.

Then, finally, after many months of constant prayer and tedious paperwork, they found the parents of their future son. This teenage couple (Melinda and David) didn't plan to get married, but Melinda also didn't want to have an abortion. It was her idea to give the baby up for adoption.

All the parents of kids in Anna's class celebrated as she and John began the exciting journey of preparing for their future son. They already knew that they would call him Ruben.

Anna and John were involved in every step of Melinda's prenatal care. They visited the doctor with her and even kept a scrapbook to one day give Ruben about how they had planned for his birth. Our whole school threw Anna a huge baby shower to outfit the nursery they were preparing. As Melinda's due date neared, Anna and John were giddy to finally bring Ruben into their home.

But the adoption was complicated. David's parents were angry about Melinda's decision. David was an only child, and they wanted a grandson. Over and over, they offered to raise Ruben on their own. And over and over, David explained to his parents that this wasn't their decision. Or even his. He and Melinda had broken up, and she wanted Anna and John to be Ruben's parents.

And, then, with Melinda's due date just a few weeks away, David was in a catastrophic car accident. He shattered part of his skull, and the damage to his brain was permanent.

Ruben came into the world right after the accident, when David's parents were hurting and frantic and upset. In the span of a month, they realized that their only son would never be the same again and therefore they had lost their only chance at having a grandson. More than ever, they wanted to raise Ruben.

Melinda had gone into labor on March 18, and John and Anna brought Ruben home on March 20, the first day of spring. All of the parents of Anna's students took turns visiting the new family with casseroles and gifts. Anna and John were so in love with everything about their new son—from his cute toes, to his dreamy blue eyes, to his head full of curly black hair. Anna snuggled and kissed him, so thankful God had given them this sweet blessing.

Then, on Good Friday (within the allotted ten days for the birth mother to change her mind), David's parents presented Anna and John with a written statement claiming custody of Ruben.

Anna and John were shocked. Melinda had suddenly changed her mind and decided that Ruben's best home environment would be with the birth father's parents. Over the Easter weekend, as Anna and John tried to celebrate the resurrection of their Savior, they were also mourning the dark reality that they were losing their son. Their grief was unspeakable.

To say they were heartbroken would be an understatement. For the months following Ruben's new placement, Anna's faith felt damaged. Even today, John struggles to talk about what happened. Why would God give them this son and then take him away? Every angle of this seemed cruel. How was *this* a caring God?

But Anna and John's story was far from over. God was preparing them for a new miracle.

Anna and John's struggle with faith and healing continued for several months. Counseling and prayer and a returned investment into the world of adoption became their norm. There were even additional losses along the way as they continued to cry out to God and seek His will for the growth of their family.

Then when it seemed like hope was almost gone—a miracle occurred. Anna was pregnant.

She was shocked and overjoyed and guarded. Throughout Anna's pregnancy, she and John were terrified this would end in another heartbreak. Every day, every waking hour, they prayed for God to bless her pregnancy and to care for their baby.

On Easter Sunday, exactly a year later, Anna gave birth to a perfectly healthy, adorable baby boy named Samuel. He is truly their miracle baby—what some moms who have lost pregnancies call a "rainbow baby."

After so many storms of miscarriages and the loss of Ruben, God showed Anna and John that He had been caring for them the whole time. Baby Samuel was their rainbow, their dove carrying an olive branch. Their storm waters were receding. They had their son.

The lessons that Anna and John learned through their adoption and the loss of Ruben have never left them. They still pray for their first son every day, and Anna says that she will always love Ruben.

Today, Anna and John are two of the happiest parents I have ever seen. At church or Wednesday night family Bible studies, Anna and John beam at Samuel. To merely glance at them is to see joy and wonderment on their faces.

Samuel is not at all what they expected for their family. And yet, he is the perfect Easter reminder of God's faithfulness.

THE PRICE OF PRIDE

Over the past fourteen years, I've spoken to my little sister only two times: to tell her our grandma had died and that my son had been born.

Do I miss her? Sometimes.

But now it's like a dull ache, like when I let myself think about how sad it is that I've never met my nieces. Or if I see someone from when we were little, I hate admitting we don't talk to my sister anymore. I always tell those people too much about what happened—about how she chose to not be part of our family.

To be really honest, the problems with my family were always there. When my sister and I were young, we were army brats and we moved a lot. Even then, she could be so negative. You could get her in a good mood if you joked with her or agreed with her, but we all got tired of doing that.

I kept waiting for her to grow up and just decide to be happy. But things had to go her way or she pouted.

I think my sister probably wishes we had more of a relationship now too. After she would have a temper tantrum, she would always be so sorry.

I think we're all sorry right now.

—Brad, 44

Those who live according to the flesh set their minds on the things of the flesh, but those who live according to the Spirit set their minds on the things of the Spirit. For to set the mind on the flesh is death, but to set the mind on the Spirit is life and peace. For the mind that is set on the flesh is hostile to God, for it does not submit to God's law; indeed, it cannot. Those who are in the flesh cannot please God.

You, however, are not in the flesh but in the Spirit, if in fact the Spirit of God dwells in you.   *Romans 8:5–9*

Not Big Huggers

M y friend Rosie is a gorgeous, fun, sweet, big-hearted fourth-generation Houstonian. She makes us all laugh with her cute sayings. (Recently, to a friend who had just moved to Texas and hadn't bought a toll tag yet: "Are you serious? The toll roads are the only way to beat Houston traffic. In a month, you'll have a toll tag on your *bike*.") Rosie loves margaritas in every flavor, spicy Tex-Mex, slow-smoked brisket, crawfish, her church, and laughing. ("In our family, having a sense of humor is as important as having a pulse.") She has pretty red hair, wide hips, and gets a manicure twice a week. Rosie always smells like Chanel and hugs everyone. We all love Rosie.

When they were in college, Rosie's husband fell for her passion for life. And she loved the quiet way he could handle anything. Ryan was the opposite of Rosie in every way. He was from a small, serious family in Maine. His dad was a banker, and his mom stayed at home to raise Ryan and keep an immaculate house.

Ryan's parents had strict ideas about everything, from the best time to eat dinner (5:30), to what should be on the table (meat, starch, veggies, and milk), to who should be around it (only family, not friends at mealtimes).

Rosie would entertain us with stories about her rigid mother-in-law and severe father-in-law. In Rosie's words, "Let's just say they're not big huggers." How had our loud, big-hearted Rosie ended up in this straitlaced family?

But Rosie desperately wanted her new in-laws to love her. She showed up for every visit with her in-laws like a golden retriever panting for attention. "Like me! Accept me! Adore me!" Yet her mother-in-law always asked Rosie passive-aggressive questions like, "Ryan isn't concerned about the money you spend? Don't you find women who work outside the home to be harsh? Doesn't Ryan miss having real maple syrup all the way down here in Texas?"

When Rosie got pregnant with their first baby, she was nervous about her mother-in-law becoming a bigger part of their lives. One day she told me, "The doctor says this baby will only weigh seven pounds, but I think it will be more like a two-hundred-pound rhino for how much it will turn our family inside out."

After Baby Sadie arrived, Rosie's mother-in-law came to help out. At the Sip and See we had for Rosie and Sadie, her mother-in-law told each of us that she really hoped Rosie would quit her job and stay home to raise Sadie.

Even as Ryan's mom ranted about the "disgusting germs" at day care, we could also sense her fear. She had stayed at home with her baby because she thought that was best, and now she wanted the best for her new granddaughter too.

Unfortunately for Rosie—and the future of her relationship with her mother-in-law—everyone's opinion was doused with a whole lot of toxic pride.

Think about what has happened when a new baby has come into your family. How did the new addition rearrange everyone's positions? How did this also awaken everyone's pride—their opinions plus their self-righteousness?

_____

_____

_____

_____

WISE COUNSEL—AND LOTS OF LETTERS

Sadie is now ten, and Rosie and her mother-in-law have just barely survived a decade-long war. There have been silent treatments, snapping at each other, and passive-aggressive comments about everything from whether women should work to how many layers Sadie should wear when she plays in the New England snow.

A couple of years ago, I saw Rosie and Sadie in the grocery store, and Rosie filled me in on the most recent drama happening with her mother-in-law. As

I listened, I glanced at pretty, polite Sadie. She's blonde and very much like Ryan, a quiet, careful girl. Even though she said little during my conversation with her mom, I imagined that Sadie was secretly hoping her mom and her grandma would figure this out.

To Sadie, their pride must have felt like cancer, with metastases spreading throughout the family tree and threatening to cut off whole limbs. If these old branches couldn't work out their issues, the whole tree was coming down. Sadie must have been hoping the strong, sturdy limbs wouldn't spread their poison to her.

When Ryan's dad died, he told Rosie that his mom couldn't handle the Northeastern winters on her own. Ryan insisted that she live in their spare bedroom from Thanksgiving until Valentine's Day every year. Even though Rosie couldn't argue with her husband's sweet care for his mom, she also couldn't stand a winter living with his mother's disapproval and tirades about things like why Sadie shouldn't be allowed to wear high heels.

Ryan did what he had always done. He did his best to take care of both his mom and Rosie. He tried not to take sides. He also asked the discipleship pastor at their church to meet with his mom and wife every other week. He gave the same direction to both women he loved, "For me, please learn to live with each other."

The meetings with the pastor ("cold war briefings" is what Rosie called them) were hard and awkward. Rosie reported that she was too eager. Her mother-in-law kept her lips pursed and gave one-word replies. (Pastor: "How are things going at your house?" Rosie: "Really good! I feel like we're making progress and I'm so grateful!" Mother-in-law: "Fine.")

Rosie said that things back at home weren't actually going that well. She said, "It's still the Civil War playing out in our kitchen every morning." Inside her mind ran a constant radio station of everything offensive Ryan's mom did: refusing to eat jambalaya and making herself toast instead, commenting loudly and frequently if Rosie had a second (or third) glass of wine, snubbing Rosie's own mother at Sadie's soccer games.

At the start of the session, Pastor Schmidt would read them a Bible verse, and then they would talk about what they could learn from the text. Rosie said the lesson was always about not having too much pride. ("If you're stubborn, that's pride. If you're easily irritated, that's pride. If you need a lot of attention, pride again. If you're often offended, that's pride too.") Rosie said she just shouted, "Pride!" every time the pastor asked a question. Clearly, he had decided that was the problem in Rosie's house.

The pastor asked the women to write letters apologizing for all the times they had done any of these to each other. "Dear Mother-in-Law, I'm sorry for assuming you would offend me . . . I was being proud." and "Please forgive me for not speaking to you on Wednesday. My feelings were hurt and so was my pride." and "I apologize for not considering what you like to eat. I was being proud."

Ryan's mom tried with the letters too. In her plain print, she wrote short notes addressed to Rosie. She apologized for not liking her cooking, for complaining about how hot they kept the house, and for criticizing Rosie when she didn't take Sophie to the doctor for what turned out to be strep throat.

But then last month, the pastor mixed it up a bit. I guess the letters weren't working. He made Rosie write a letter to herself from her mother-in-law's point of view. Her mother-in-law had to write one from Rosie's point of view.

And it was these letters that changed everything.

For each symptom of pride, write how you've been guilty of this:

1. Acting stubborn: _____

_____

2. Being easily irritated: _____

_____

3. Needing lots of attention/affirmation: _____

_____

4. Often being offended: _____

_____

Pray for God to help you to see these symptoms of pride and confess that they hurt your relationships, especially the relationships in your family.

THE TOXIC METASTASES OF PRIDE

As I've been following Rosie's story from the sidelines, I've also been writing this book about how families can build a culture of grace—and what can poison that culture. In both the process of writing this book and Rosie's relationship with her mother-in-law, I was learning how pride kills the buds of grace.

I started to understand this right about the time the letters started to work between Rosie and her mother-in-law. Rosie said that somehow the idea of writing from her mother-in-law's point of view tricked her into feeling compassion for the older woman. Rosie said that writing from her mother-in-law's point of view also made her understand Ryan's mom as a scared and helpless woman. Actually, these letters helped Rosie to see her mother-in-law a little like God probably sees her—so needy for love and affection.

Rosie began to see herself like this too, as vulnerable, as hungry for love and affection. She said she was beginning to understand more and more how much grace she had received. Grace from Ryan. Grace from his mom. From Sadie. Most of all, from God. Rosie said, "When I see myself from this other perspective, I look spoiled. Like I was born on third base and then feeling so good about myself because I got a home run. Who am I, really? I'm just blessed. I'm learning to be grateful for what I have. Really, I didn't earn any of this."

When I sat down with Rosie last week, this is what she reported. "I realized that I have been a little crazy when it comes to getting my own way. When it comes to Sadie, I'm really crazy. But through those letters, something kind of tugged free in me so I could totally see why I can drive my mother-in-law and husband crazy. Then what do you know, everything just kind of blew up in my head, like a building had exploded or something. All the pride and control and all of it. That's when I knew I was doomed, because, suddenly, I felt sorry for my mother-in-law. Then I kind of liked her for putting up with me for so long. I realized that she had been doing the best she could. So, yeah, there's that. Crazy, huh?"

How does pride hurt your relationship with God? Think of Eve, who wanted to be like God. How did pride cause her to eat the forbidden fruit? What about your faith right now? How does pride prevent you from understanding your need for a Savior?

The Best Spiritual Truth for the Rest of Your Life

Let's call Rosie's realization the Spiritual Truth of Low Expectations.

This is the realization that every other person (even your family members . . . *especially* your family members) is made of the same ego and clumsiness and rage and self-righteousness that caused World War II and slavery and mean Facebook comments. They are all made up of the same sin. This sin is pride and control and hate, and it's surprising and it's awful. And yet, this is all part of human relationships.

As we try to build a culture of grace in our own home, I explain it to my kids in the simplest terms: sometimes giving grace to other people feels a lot like having low expectations and a bad memory.

A culture of grace means letting your sister off the hook for taking the last package of fruit snacks, or for borrowing your flip-flops without asking, or for teasing you when you didn't know how to say "hi" in Spanish, for calling the muffins you made "nasty," for slamming the car door on your finger, for telling everyone at school you still sleep with a stuffed Snoopy.

Yes, your sister might really be at fault for most of these. Yes, the parents will sort out responsibility and punishments. Of course your sister will be held accountable for her actions. But for you—for your heart—quickly let go of your anger with her. Don't take her sins personally against you. Instead, realize that she is sinful, as are you, as are we all.

We are usually just acting out that sin, and we need radical forgiveness for that. Don't hold on to your pride and bitterness for months. Instead, realize that the carelessness and evil and hatred you see in me is also in you. Instead, pray to forgive wholeheartedly.

I've found this works with our kids. They understand that forgiveness over pride is a choice. They like the idea of calling this "low expectations and a very bad memory."

Quick forgiveness is what Rosie eventually learned about living with her mother-in-law, and this is what you can learn about living with your family. Sin really is that horrible and it really is in all of us. Recognizing that is the first step in extending grace to everyone.

Pick a family member, any family member. Write that person's name here. Now write one expectation you have for him or her. "I expect her to always return my texts. I expect him to stop drinking after a couple beers. I expect their family to appreciate the time and energy I give them."

Now scratch through the expectation you've written. You can even draw a cross over this name and expectation. Finally, pray about your relationship with this family member. Ask God to help you to communicate better, but also for you to forgive quickly.

_____

_____

_____

_____

SPOILER ALERT: THE FLESH WILL ABSOLUTELY ALWAYS DISAPPOINT US

But, really, why are we so surprised by the toxicity of sin? God is pretty clear throughout the Bible that it's the worst stuff we can imagine. It's mixed into our souls and psyches in such indelible ways that we see everything through the horrible, cloudy lenses of this sludge.

Sin is like MSG. The more of it we taste, the more we crave. Our greed and pride and need to control can and will run rampant through our minds, souls, lives, and families.

You and I and everyone lusts after more money, more power, more empty adoration, more things we can have delivered to our doors in just a couple days, more cake and things we can stuff in our mouths and in our carts. More of everything our flesh craves. We expect all of these to provide deep satisfaction. And they never deliver. Quick pleasure, yes. A quick, delicious taste, yes.

But the adoration fades, the new stuff rots, being right loses its appeal, the control was just a myth.

Of course, the wonderful news in this equation is that this is the beginning of finally understanding that it's God who is worthy of our craving. God keeps pursuing us; He gives us tastes of His love and our souls are quenched. This is the good stuff. We know there is Something here that lasts. That Something is a real Savior.

The apostle Paul wrote about the difference between the sinful things we lust after and a real Savior in Romans 8:5. "For those who live according to the flesh set their minds on the things of the flesh, but those who live according to the Spirit set their minds on the things of the Spirit."

To explain the point further, Paul speaks this horrible, beautiful truth, "To set the mind on the flesh is death, but to set the mind on the Spirit is life and peace" (Romans 8:6).

You can probably point to a painful season when you've learned this to be true about a life of the flesh. Anything you create with your hands, or any fantastic job offer you're dreaming of, or anything you can buy with just one click will eventually die. They were all a treadmill of pride, pride, pride. The satisfaction and temporary joy just doesn't touch the deep needs we have for real joy, deep love, genuine grace.

Most tragically, everything of actual flesh dies too. Our bodies, and the bodies of those we love, are so temporary, so perishable, so disposable, so delicate. These strong hands that earn the paycheck are getting tired. These eyes that have always noticed detail are fading. This heart that beats so rhythmically will grow weary. This body—like the clothes around it and the home protecting it and the friends and family surrounding it—will eventually die.

This sad news is exactly what Paul was warning us of those centuries ago when he gave us the instruction to live in the Spirit. That's where we will find the life and the peace that we are all searching for—Jesus.

He's what we were looking for all along.

Paul teaches us that flesh dies and things of the flesh die too. Make a list of flesh things you've trusted. Write how those have disappointed you. Why, then, do you still crave more of these? How is life in the Spirit different?

_____

_____

_____

_____

But YES to the Spirit!

A life in the Spirit often feels like deep vulnerability.

Living as a child of God includes the experience of reading a Bible verse that your soul leaps at because, in your most tender places, you know it as truth. Life in the Spirit is humbling; it's recognizing the radical patience and kindness another person has shown you. Life in the Spirit is praying to your Father and feeling the profound peace that comes from knowing He is taking care of you and has been caring for you. Life in the Spirit is hearing an explanation of God's expansive love for you that resonates so deeply that you feel whole. Life in the Spirit is receiving the undeserved forgiveness of someone you have hurt.

This vulnerability—this experiencing of a life in the Spirit while still sinful—is your dual citizenship. It's your identity as God's child that trumps your identity as a human son or mother or sister or aunt. God's love is eternal and unbreakable and healing and transformative. This love is perfect. Never, ever will this love run out. The peace you feel after Communion is from tasting this faith, from tasting God's love and Jesus' sacrifice.

This is _it_. This is the real and powerful love that we share with our family when we build a culture of grace.

Living by the Spirit means peace, just like Paul said. When you're lit like this with peace from the inside, it shines to the outside. When you're relating to other people on a soul level, no one is expecting too much of one another's flesh. Instead, you are sharing the fruits of the Spirit, the love of our Savior, and the new olive branches of our Father.

Yes. This, my friends. This exactly. Living the life of the Spirit. This is the place of incredibly low expectations of the flesh. This is the place of God's grace.

Maybe we could live here with our families? Maybe here we could connect as God's children instead of as the hurting humans of flesh?

Have you ever had this experience of connecting to someone in your family on a spiritual level? How does this feel like peace multiplied and pride subtracted? Write the story here.

_____

_____

_____

_____

Low Expectations in Action

It was early January, right after the saccharine rush of the holidays, when everyone was feeling more than a little hungover from spending so much money and binge eating fudge and biting their tongues at so many family gatherings.

My friend Georgia (one of my all-time favorite people) met me for lunch. Georgia is wonderful because she has mastered the art of expecting very little from other people. She says she has a low tolerance for drama, but it's more than that. She accepts all of us in our unfinished, half-baked states. If you forget to return her text or her muffin tins for six months, she just laughs and tells you the muffin tins are now yours. She's one of the happiest people I know.

While we shared a platter of barbecue nachos, Georgia told me about Christmas with her parents and her two older brothers. Just a couple days before Christmas, Georgia had discovered that her brother—the black sheep of the family—had secretly arranged for Georgia to pay for his storage unit for a year.

For years, the two of them had rented units at the same big storage company. Georgia and her family used the extra space to store Christmas decorations and off-season clothes. Her brother, who was in between apartments and living with his parents, used his storage unit to store his leather sectional.

Her brother had gone into the office at the storage place and changed his unit to her name. He had forged the documents and—amazingly—successfully conned everyone into believing his sister was now responsible for his bill.

Georgia had paid for both storage units for a year before she looked closely at the bill and discovered what her brother had done.

Then she had to figure out how to deal with the $3,000 he owed her.

Instead of emailing her family a manifesto about what a danger this brother was to the family or refusing to show up at Christmas or tattling to their mom about it all, Georgia wrote her brother a letter—on a copy of the storage bill. The letter said, "Dear brother . . . Merry Christmas. I'm glad I could help you out, but please ask next time. Love, Georgia."

This move flabbergasted me. Georgia had missed out on so much: her moment of righteous indignation; her extra credit with her parents; wallowing in her own goodness; being outraged by her brother's small, black, stealing heart. She had missed out on the pride fest her brother owed her.

But, as Georgia pointed out, she also missed out on the truly pointless drama. As we polished off the nachos, she said, "Really, what good is it to show off about being better than my brother? I'm not that great myself."

Low expectations. Humbleness. Quick forgiveness. Patience and radical kindness. Gratitude for her family. Love that's not self-serving. Seeing her family through the eyes of the Spirit instead of eyes of flesh.

Bam!

Put yourself in Georgia's place. What would you have done if your brother had stolen from you like this? What would have fueled this reaction for you? Pride? The need to be right? How is this arrogance lethal to olive branches in your family?

_____

_____

_____

_____

And Sometimes You Feel Like Big Bird on Skis

This week, we traveled with another family to Breckenridge, Colorado, for a week of skiing. My husband and the other couple are competent athletes and expert skiers. I am not. When I stand at the top of the mountain, I feel like Big Bird perched on two slim sticks, staring downhill.

Our kids quickly learned to ski, and they all traversed down the mountain like fearless snow bunnies. My husband was gleeful as he circled us all on his snowboard, helping kids try jumps and navigate trees. Mike and the kids looked like a Swiss Family Robinson sequel, in which they try out for the Olympic ski team. I looked like a physics experiment that successfully proved gravity. I was also doing an excellent job of demonstrating the scientific law that a body in motion will continue to tumble right down the mountain if not stopped by a tree.

As I crashed and fell and stopped, I chanted to myself the undeniable truth, "I am terrible at this. I am terrible. I'm too scared and too clumsy and too tall and too out of shape. I am holding everyone else back." To my family, I waved and smiled and yelled encouragement. "You're all naturals!" I reminded them as they disappeared over the next hill.

At lunch, my twelve-year-old daughter said, "Mommy, we're tired of always waiting for you. Would it be okay if we did some harder slopes—without you?"

Tears sprang to my eyes, and I sort of wanted to kick her with my ski boot. But she was right. They were all ready for more challenging runs, and I needed to stay back with the ski school groups.

Then, Mike put his hand on my knee. "We don't care if you're good at skiing or not. We like having you with us on the mountain." He looked at the kids. "It's more fun with Mommy there, isn't it?"

They all agreed. Nate chimed in that he loves how I always have lip balm in my pocket for him. Our twins, Sam and Elisabeth, thought I was funny. Even Catie agreed that it was the most fun to have an adventure with all of us together.

This is the one-two punch of grace. My family saw the truth about me (Big Bird on skis) and they accepted me for it (we want you with us anyway). Mike didn't expect me to zip down the slopes, navigating moguls. He had (rightfully) low expectations for my skiing skills. But he still accepted me because he loves me.

Paul was so good at explaining this specific one-two blessing of grace. In Ephesians 2:8–10, he writes, "For by grace you have been saved through faith. And *this is not your own doing; it is the gift of God,* not a result of works, so that no one may boast. For we are His workmanship, created in Christ Jesus for good works, which God prepared beforehand, that we should walk in them" (emphasis added).

This is the bittersweet truth of grace. God saved you because He loves you. And there's zero, zilch, absolutely nothing you can do to earn it. He sees you like Big Bird on skis—clumsy and terrible at loving your family. You can't pretend to be any different because God always knows exactly who you are.

Second, God accepts you in your clumsiness. He wants you with Him because He loves you. He cares for you and helps you care for your family. God wants you to be with Him because you are His child. You can keep trying to ski better or more beautifully or faster, and He'll love you just the same.

And then, some days, you'll just fall over in the snow, too weary to keep trying.

God will be right there with you.

He never will have left you.

Look at Ephesians 2:8–10 and meditate on the incredibly good news that you do not have to do anything or be anything more for your heavenly Father to accept you. In light of this good news, what struggle or attempt to prove can you release? How might this connect you more deeply with your identity in Christ?

_____

_____

_____

_____

Low Expectations ≠ No Discipline

As you build a culture of grace in your family, low expectations does not mean you should be afraid to discipline your kids. Actually, it means quite the opposite. Parents give their kids rules out of love, to protect them, to help them take responsibility for their own actions, and to reinforce their worth.

If you jump on your bed, you'll sit in a time-out. If you continue to do it, we'll move your bed into the hallway until we feel like you're ready to have the responsibility again. If you fail a math test, you'll go to after-school tutoring instead of going to the park with the rest of us. We love you too much to let you ride on the back of the neighbor boy's motorcycle. #sorrynotsorry #youcanwalk

Even though Mike and I are in our forties, our parents still discipline us. Recently, he had a health scare and didn't call his parents to tell them what had happened. His mom pulled him aside and said, "I know you don't like to make a big deal out of stuff like this, but we want to know what's going on so we can pray for you. If you find yourself in the ER, that would be a very good time to call your mother."

Here is where we can look to our heavenly Father for a model of how perfect, unconditional love and discipline look. God has boundaries, expectations, and discipline for us. God was very clear that the Ten Commandments were not the Ten Suggestions.

And then Jesus showed and told us what a Christian life should look like. We can see that we fall short of all of this. We are God's children who are trying to follow His rules, but we keep messing up. We fail, hit back, make gods out of everything, and live entirely for ourselves.

Just like my relationship with my kids, just like my relationship with my parents, the underlying current is forgiveness and reconciliation. Yes, you lost child, you didn't do it all perfectly. Even you, achievement-loving child, you didn't do it perfectly either. But it's not about your success or failure. It's about your membership as part of this family. It's about acceptance and love. It's about confession. It's about forgiveness.

Over and over, this is the message of Scripture. God shows us that our acceptance into His family is not about being Jew or Gentile. It's not about keeping the Commandments. It's not about how your outside looks at all. It's about your soul, His love, and your adoption as His child.

This is the kind of unconditional love I want our kids to know and understand fully. You are not loved because you follow our rules or because you show up to church or you smile for the family pictures. None of that really makes a difference.

In a culture of grace, you are loved because of your status as our child, and that is sacred. God gave us you, and there is absolutely nothing you can do to separate yourself from us or to lose this identity. There's also nothing you can do to improve that status. We will love, encourage, discipline, and take care of you. Just as you are a fully accepted and celebrated child of God, you are also our child.

Forever and ever. Amen.

Talk about rules and obedience in your family right now. List three rules you have for your kids or for the next generation. How are these high expectations? How does forgiveness, when they fall short, show the concept of low expectations?

_____

_____

_____

_____

PRUNING YOUR FAMILY TREE

The opposite of the vulnerability we find in the Spirit is the hardened hearts we find in the flesh. These fights remind me of the three sisters I met when I spoke at a recent prayer breakfast. Two of the sisters (and their husbands) had been members at the same church for forty years. The third sister was divorced, and she attended another church in the same town. Once a year, the churches worked together to host a big women's event. The two sisters who attended the same church were close friends. They raised their kids, and now their grandkids, side by side. One of these sisters was in charge of the food, and the other was the head of the table decorating.

The next generation, one of the daughters of these two women, helped me set up a table to sell my books. And—just as it always happens when women work together—we chatted. As we set out books and hung signs, she told me what had happened years ago between her mom and aunts, a story about how pride had spread herbicide all over the roots of her family tree.

Two decades before, the two sisters who went to the same church decided to take their kids to Disney World together. Because the third sister didn't have kids yet (and because her husband could be overbearing), they didn't invite her along. This hurt the third sister so deeply that she didn't speak to the two sisters for years. She didn't contact them when she went through a divorce from that overbearing man. And she didn't call them after she was in a serious car accident. She didn't even speak to her sisters, or her nieces, at the yearly prayer breakfast. Even as they all gathered in this same room together, broke banana bread side by side, and asked God to bless their relationships, the sisters turned away from each other.

"What?" I stopped unpacking books to look at my new friend. This was terrible news. "Oh no," I said. "That's exactly what I'm talking about here today—about forgiving your family. At the end of my talk, the women are supposed to pray about showing grace to one another."

I had hoped for the prayer time to be powerful, an opportunity for family members to ask God for olive branches in their own trees.

But the daughter laughed. "You know what will happen?" she asked. "My mom and her sister will pray about forgiveness—only they will pray that my aunt realizes she's hard-hearted. They will tell the whole table about the fight." She rolled her eyes. "They are so far into this fight, it's the only way they can see it."

Well, awesome. This was not ideal. My plan had been for the women coming today to find comfort in the prayer time, and for the Holy Spirit to nudge them toward reconciliation with difficult family relationships. I wasn't looking for a gossip session about a decades-old spat.

In the end, the third sister didn't show up to the breakfast. Not only that, the other two sisters were so busy setting up food that they weren't even part of the prayer time.

So, even though all three sisters avoided the potential awkwardness and gossip, they also missed out on the powerful moments of spiritual insight. Maybe even real forgiveness within their family tree.

And it's that very family tree—the future generations—that will suffer from the self-righteousness of these prideful roots. In the cyclical, sprawling life of families, the actions of your ancestors always stay part of your family's identity. If you build a culture of grace with low expectations for one another and eyes of forgiveness, your grandchildren will reap the rewards of this spiritual transformation.

The same is true if you allow bitterness and arrogance to rule in your family. If you stop speaking to your son or your sister, you teach these lessons of conceit and isolation to your kids. If you live by the flesh—believing that being right is more important than love or forgiveness—you will discover that this is also the lesson you're teaching them all.

Long after I had left that church in that town, I thought about my new friend, the niece of an aunt she had never really known. What had this woman learned about how to handle conflict? How had this self-righteousness formed parts of her personality? And—because this is almost always the way family works—what had she taught her own daughters about how to treat their sisters?

> When we don't resolve conflict quickly, it can fester. Like an infected limb, it can poison the whole body, the whole tree. Tell the story of a conflict in your life that started small, but then spread unchecked throughout your whole life. What damage did this do?

_____

_____

_____

_____

JESUS' PLAN TO RESOLVE CONFLICT

Because Jesus is 100 percent Man, He saw the fist-to-fist, hurtful word-to-hurtful-word drama of conflict play out in real life.

But because Jesus is also totally God, His commands about how to resolve fights come from a place of unconditional love for His people. In other words, when our teaching, healing, foot-washing Savior says *anything* about human conflict, it's a very good idea to lean in.

First, Jesus instructed us to resolve conflict quickly (see Matthew 5:23–25). Actually, quick resolution is often our good first instinct when we argue with a family member. When my husband snaps at me or, for instance, lets the kids watch the movie we agreed they shouldn't see, my first nudge is to talk to him before the pride and hurt feelings grab my soul. My instinct is to say, "Hey. Are you okay?" Or "Is there something I'm missing about the movie?"

But when I let the bitterness seep into my thoughts, and my self-righteousness is off and running, I'm suddenly remembering EVERY SINGLE

TIME he has ever snapped at me. The instinct to forgive is gone and replaced by a mental montage of all his past transgressions.

Back to the women at the prayer breakfast, I wonder what would have happened if they had resolved the conflict quickly? What if, all those years ago, when the third sister heard about the trip, her first instinct had been to call her sisters and say, "The trip you're planning hurts my feelings. I feel rejected and left out"? What if then, their first instinct had been to say, "Oh no. We weren't rejecting you at all. This vacation involves mostly kids' activities. But maybe we could work together to find a way you would enjoy it too"?

In the Sermon on the Mount, Jesus said that if you're angry with your brother or sister, God sees you as a murderer. So, clearly, moving past anger is a big deal to our heavenly Father. Obviously, He doesn't want us nursing old hurts. He understands that our human hearts can easily become little jewel boxes to treasure our hate. Treasuring our hate is the exact opposite of what God wants for our hearts.

Ephesians 4:26 instructs you to not let the sun go down on your anger. When you stay angry day after day, it's a trick. You feel like you are doing the right thing. You believe that going to bed hurt is the best way to move forward. You tell yourself that you are so good at closing doors, and that is the absolute best way to move on.

But then, what you realize eventually is that this is not the way it works with closed doors. After a couple days of hearing your own shrill voice in your head, you understand that the phone calls are coming from inside the house.

You've locked yourself up with your own mind—and it terrorizes you. The angry, bitter thoughts replay over and over right in your own head. You can't shake loose your own broken record of how right, right, right you are. You are drinking the rat poison and expecting the rat to die.

Holding on to hate damages you psychologically, emotionally, and physically. Your conceited anger, when you store it up in your heart, becomes the worst poison to you. This is why so much of what Jesus taught and God insists we do is based on love and grace and getting rid of pride.

Your heavenly Father loves you and takes care of you. He doesn't want you drinking the deadly concoction of arrogance and hatred. Instead, He wants you to listen to His commands and share love and grace with the people you struggle with the most: your own family.

Talk about this idea that your own anger and self-righteousness are the real punishment. When someone you love hurts your feelings, do you find yourself harboring your anger toward them, replaying their sins over and over? Write how this can be its own punishment.

_____

_____

_____

_____

Face-to-Face (Not Facebook-to-Facebook)

Next, Jesus says we should resolve conflict directly, face-to-face (see Matthew 18:15).

It's as if He knew that texting would be invented in the next couple thousand years. Or voicemail. Or tweeting. And it's like He could see the horrible conflict that would come with this era of people not talking face-to-face.

Of course, He totally knew all of that was coming. He also knew that all these nondirect communications would become fertile ground where we would bury our worst grudges.

The difference between telling someone face-to-face that your feelings are hurt and texting them is the difference between kissing and reading about a kiss. One is powerful and intimate. The other is bland and indirect and an incredibly poor substitute. Which is EXACTLY why most of us do this kind of passive-aggressive garbage—because it sidesteps so much of our fear and avoids so much of our own inner _cringiness_.

In Matthew 18:15, Jesus also says we should handle conflict one-on-one. Anyone who has survived seventh grade absolutely knows the wisdom in this. Spreading your hate around through gossip is damaging on so many levels. Because when you tell the story of My Unfair Rejection or How I Was Insulted, you never tell it quite accurately.

Talking face-to-face dissipates much of the drama from the conflict. This is because the two people talking are also the two who know what really did and did not happen. Face-to-face is genius in its effectiveness to resolve conflict.

Also, face-to-face discussions leave no room for slander. Or for what almost went down in the fellowship hall at the prayer breakfast—the Christian's version of gossip: "Can you pray for my sister, who is awful and small-hearted and struggles with pride and has been mad at us for two decades? Thanksverymuch!"

Finally, Jesus tells us to get help to resolve the conflict (see Matthew 18:16–17). He doesn't say, "If you've tried my first couple of ideas, and they don't work, then that's fine. In fact, that's more than fine! That's great news. For your hard work at trying to resolve conflict, you get a first-class ticket to Martyrdom. This is a super fun land for your brain, pride, ego, and self-righteousness. Here, your imagination gets to run wild on all the roller coasters of Wounded Thoughts and Finding the Other Person's Character Flaws. Stay in Martyrdom forever because this is where everything is under your control. You can eat deep-fried butter on a stick all day and imagine it doesn't affect your health at all. You rule in this place!"

Unfortunately for our pride, Jesus' message is more one of "If both you and the other injured party can't agree on what's wrong, why not ask someone who isn't feeding their own hungry ego (i.e., one or two others) to come along?"

What do you think would have happened if those two sisters had asked their husbands to come along and talk it out with the outcast sister? Maybe disaster. Or maybe these guys would have shared a few thoughts about what they realized was an ugly ball of misunderstanding, conceit, and plain old hurt feelings?

Or what about the next generation, the children in these families? My new friend rolled her eyes as she told me about her mom and aunt. If only she could have talked as openly with them as she talked with me, the women might have listened. The next generation might have been a voice of reason in this pride-fueled feud.

In today's culture, it's so tempting to confront another person over text or even over the phone. What has been your experience with this? What benefits have you discovered come from talking face-to-face?

_____

_____

Take Your Family Problems to Church

Finally, Jesus says that we should tell our arguments to the church (see Matthew 18:17). Yes, this can make for some awkward moments. And I can't say that I would have handled it well if my talk about family forgiveness had ended with one of the sisters standing up in that crowded fellowship hall telling her side of the Great-Disney-Trip-Misunderstanding from twenty years before.

Or maybe this would have been one of those wonderful Holy Spirit moments. Maybe this would have prompted a discussion or a confession. And saying this aloud in front of so many friends and family members would have been the heart-changing moment from the Holy Spirit. Perhaps all those praying hearts would have been the exact moment when the Holy Spirit opened up their souls to real forgiveness. Actually, now that I think back to that day, perhaps this is the prod both women were ignoring by concentrating so hard on the fruit salad arrangement.

The most interesting (and compelling) part of Jesus' instruction about conflict resolution in Matthew 18:17 is this: If that other person refuses to listen, even to the church, treat him or her like you would a pagan or a tax collector. Walk away.

Remember, only God can change hearts. And this is God Himself telling you that if you've tried—really tried—you might discover it's time to stop bloodying your hands and heart on this argument. You can't control another person into being happy with you or close to you again. So you're free from it. Brush the dust from your feet.

Most important, see that all of these steps to resolve conflict are glittering with the very pretty grace that Jesus always sprinkled everywhere. Grace for the hurting. Grace to remove the infection that would eat up your family tree. Grace for you, the one who would bind yourself up in your own ropes of superiority. Grace to the future generations of your family, who will benefit so much from a culture of grace now.

Over and over, the heart of our Savior's message here on Earth was the same: grace from God to share with one another. And He even gives us detailed steps about how to do it.

Wow.

_____

_____

_____

_____

THE BOOK: *ALL THE FAMILY MEMBERS YOU DON'T HAVE TO FORGIVE*

I've been thinking about writing a Bible study called *All the Family Members You Don't Have to Forgive*. Except I'm pretty sure no one would buy a copy. Or maybe lots of people would—and that would be a terrible steroid shot to all of our own egos. Perhaps the better concept would be a book called *The Secret to Happy Families Is to Realize Everyone Will Be Very Bad at Taking Care of One Another*.

Or better still, *Grace: God Shares His Best (Try to Spread It Around)*.

Let's look at the grace part. It's our only hope this side of heaven.

To review, so far we've learned that our family is where we find most of our earthly identity. This is sacred business we are working at together, and it's all so very delicate. What you do as a mother and a son and how you treat your brother has implications that can affect generations.

And yet, all of this isn't stressful at all. Because the truth is, what can we really expect from a bunch of whiny egomaniacs like all of us? Of course, we will get all this love and grace and forgiveness business wrong almost all of the time. We are practically expected to act only in the most self-serving and immature ways. Your family will slight you on levels you never saw coming. They will not show up when you need them—or they will and then they'll abandon you just when you started to rely on them. They will gossip and teach you all the wrong lessons about forgiveness. They will mangle unconditional love so badly, it won't even be recognizable.

And you will do this to them too.

Yet you will continue to trudge forward, trying to find ways to forgive them, and they will continue to mess up in more and more blatantly sinful ways. Then, you realize it's you who has been on the wrong path. And you will have to repent and go back for more forgiveness. More grace. They will try to forgive you, too, as you realize how you've been hurting them without even realizing it. You'll apologize and forgive and keep trying (badly) at this.

Except, then, just to confuse you even more, lots of times your family will be the loveliest people you can imagine. They will be the only ones who understand your dark humor or funny cat T-shirts and appreciation for quirky salt and pepper shakers. They will be the only ones who show up when you run out of money or patience or friends. You will love them so much that it hurts. You will be so grateful to them for putting up with your crazy self. They will love you in the exact right ways. Until it all goes wrong again.

So, let the circus rage around you; show up when you can, love people as they are, trust that this is the very best they can do. Know that God is always revealing more and more in the most surprising ways.

Then, back to the Bible, back to the Sacraments, back to begging at the cross, back to sharing God's love and forgiveness.

All of that, forever and ever. Amen.

Judy: An Olive Branch Story of Generosity in the Place of Pride

Judy is such a good southern grandma. She takes care of her four sons and her six grandkids with deep generosity, the kind that flows straight from her heavenly Father.

Judy takes care of others too. She's helped high school students all over Houston earn their GEDs. She cares for our church members by making the most delicious salsa. It's zesty and lemony with a bite of fresh onion. When we add Ms. Judy's salsa to tacos, they become feasts. Scrambled eggs taste grand enough for Santa Anna himself.

But what Judy is most known for is how she loves her family. Her sons and grandkids have called her at all hours of the night to help them. Right now, two of her sons and two of her grandsons live with her. Her kids and her grandkids trust that she will take care of them. They know she will always accept and love them.

Judy considers it one of God's greatest gifts that she has been able to help all of the branches of her family tree. When one of Judy's sons struggled with his girlfriend through an unplanned pregnancy, Ms. Judy helped them every single day in every way that she could.

The best testament to Judy's humbleness and generosity comes not from her family, though. Jodi is the single mother of Judy's grandson James. Jodi dated Judy's son and ended up pregnant when she was sixteen. Judy loved and supported Jodi through her pregnancy.

Although there are other ways Judy could have reacted to Jodi's pregnancy, she took the humblest approach. Through ups and downs, she kept extending the olive branch of love to her near daughter-in-law. She didn't accuse or hurt or blame, she helped.

Jodi says, "I love her. She saved me from an abusive family. She took me in even though I was teased at my school. She has done so much for me, I can't even begin to describe it."

Judy credits her heavenly Father for her dedication to her family. "My faith in my Lord is what keeps me going every day. It's all of the ways I hear from Him. I hear from Him through the Bible, through the sermon on Sunday, through my prayers. I believe Romans 8:31. I believe God when He says, 'If God is for me, who can be against me?' Nothing is too big for my God. Nothing."

Judy's faith has been a powerful witness to Jodi. She says, "When Judy's time comes, I will do whatever to keep this family together. She was there when I needed to talk, when I needed a safe haven, when I was having serious breakdowns, and when I was thinking about suicide. Her grandson wouldn't be here if she hadn't been who she is to me."

Judy trusts that God will give her exactly what she needs to take care of her family. She believes in a God who never isolates Himself, who will keep giving and giving. This is the kind of love Judy shares with her family. This is what love looks like in action.

Judy's grandson Zach says, "She takes care of me like no one else has. She's given me everything. I know God loves me because of my Grandma Judy."

HURRICANES OF CONFLICT

My family calls me The Princess. I hate that. They say I'm high-maintenance. If we're all trying to choose a restaurant, everyone will text, "Are you okay going to Cracker Barrel, Princess?" It's such an old joke that everyone thinks is so original.

But here's the truth . . . I'm not a princess at all. I've been through a divorce, I have a special-needs son, and I work as a teacher at his school. This is not the life of a princess.

Except to my family. They still need me to be the picky, difficult baby of the family. So everything I do seems fussy and high-maintenance to them. I've tried to talk to them about this, but when I bring it up, it seems like I'm being prissy and complaining.

My best friend is a counselor at our school, and she says that my family will probably never change. I just have to accept that.

But I don't want to. They might be stuck in who I used to be thirty years ago, but I don't want to be like that anymore.

—Kimmy, 34

And He gave the apostles, the prophets, the evangelists, the shepherds and teachers, to equip the saints for the work of ministry, for building up the body of Christ, until we all attain to the unity of the faith and of the knowledge of the Son of God, to mature manhood, to the measure of the stature of the fullness of Christ, so that we may no longer be children, tossed to and fro by the waves and carried about by every wind of doctrine, by human cunning, by craftiness in deceitful schemes. Rather, speaking the truth in love, we are to grow up in every way into Him who is the head, into Christ, from whom the whole body, joined and held together by every joint with which it is equipped, when each part is working properly, makes the body grow so that it builds itself up in love. *Ephesians 4:11–16*

The Crazy, Chaotic Beach House

I grew up on the small island of Galveston, Texas. The population was about 60,000—plus the tourists who loved our town's historic homes and miles of beach. The community was a combination of beach bums, old Texas families, and a corrupt local government. Because of the corruption, there was also so much poverty. My middle-class, devoutly Lutheran family didn't fit in with the *laissez les bons temps rouler* culture of south Texas.

So, like many religious families, we depended on the church for our social life, extended family, and leisure time. Our little congregation also had a school, where both my parents taught and my dad was the principal.

By the time I was old enough for preschool, my dad had moved on to become an insurance salesman. The new principal and his wife moved to Galveston from Illinois with their four fun, blonde daughters. Over the next decade, I would learn so much from their family about building a culture of grace.

Our new principal was a muscled, funny, tough character who had grown up on the rough side of Chicago in a big Irish family. He could whistle Beethoven, knew everything about the Bible, and prayed for anyone, right there on the spot. He was a no-nonsense drill sargent who made detention kids scrape gum off the desks. These were the days when the Fonz and *M*A*S*H* and Archie Bunker ruled television, and our principal was that kind of strong character.

His daughters were the funniest, toughest, sassiest girls, and I loved to spend the night at their house because we were in charge of ourselves. The oldest, Mary, had learned to drive a car when she was fourteen because sometimes she had to go to the gas station when her folks needed cigarettes. Cathi was next, and she was very pretty. She was one year older than me, and I looked up to her as if she were Christie Brinkley. The other two were Sasha and Kate, and they were even tougher than their older sisters.

They lived in a rambling beach house near the water, and life at their house felt as wild as the waves and blowing sand right outside their balcony. Everyone was fighting for something at their crazy old beach house.

Have you known a family with this kind of chaos? Write a few sentences about your impression of these family dynamics. Or, if this was your family, how did it feel to live in a family like this?

_____

_____

_____

_____

Disorder = Disaster?

Then, in 1983, Hurricane Alicia barreled through Galveston and demolished our principal's house. Like the rest of us, their family had evacuated to Houston for the storm. But when we returned a couple of days later, we heard the terrible news that the winds had torn down their old, rambling beach house.

Immediately, church members started to collect clothes for the family and created a schedule for them to take turns staying with us. On that terrible afternoon, when we came to see that only the concrete slab had survived, our principal stood on the beach, looking out at the calm after-the-storm water and cried. Then, he turned back to us and said, "Let's get to work." And we did.

In this stuttering, determined way, the principal's family kept moving forward. Their loss didn't paralyze them. Instead, the daughters and I spent our days combing through trash heaps, looking for treasures. We found a rattlesnake, a prosthetic leg, tons of clothes, and a refrigerator with food still in it. We even found some of their families' pictures and clothes.

It was a hard time (August with no AC in Texas was the first issue), and every family had to find ways to live without electricity, to get our roofs replaced, and repair the damage to our fences and yards.

We all prayed a lot and asked God to help us pull through. Still, no one was sure exactly what would happen to the island or the school or our principal and his family. It seemed unlikely that we could recover from this. Too much had been lost. But we prayed with them, moved them into a trailer, and worked hard to get them set up before the school year.

During this time, their family changed. I guess it was because they had lost so much. And they had to figure out their new reality. But we watched as their family leaned on one another and on God to figure out the next steps. When I spent the night there, I could feel them melting into one another, becoming a new family. They prayed together. They were growing closer.

In their new house—a small cottage near the beach that they moved into after the trailer—the tone was different. Even as a kid, I could feel it. I was at their house a lot during this time, and I saw how they changed. They softened toward one another. A new connection flowed between them. They listened to one another more. They had projects to do, and they worked together. I remember watching our principal as he gathered his family around the bags of donations from our church and thanked God for them. I could feel the deep vulnerability of them together there. It felt holy.

This family taught me what it looked like to be both flawed and forgiven. They were at every church service, right alongside the rest of us. Every time we celebrated Communion, I watched the family kneel for silent confession. The fights and arguments were gone in that holy moment of absolution. I'll never forget that picture of their family.

Much later, when I found out what makes families function well, I would understand this as being an agile family. Elastic relationships like this—the kind with grace flowing through them—withstand the test of time.

Have you known a family that was chaotic and dysfunctional—but also kind and faithful? Write about that family here. What good did you see happening in their home?

GRACE. FLEXIBILITY. TRUST IN GOD.

Eventually, though, the principal's family fell apart a little bit. The mother died from lung cancer (she had smoked since she was fourteen), and the principal remarried a much younger woman. This was during the girls' college years, and they all rebelled against their stepmom in different ways. One daughter got pregnant and immediately married, another got involved in drugs, and another rebelled by joining a country club and the Junior League. These were rough years for their family. But they came through to create a culture of grace within their family.

Surely, the childhood home of these girls had not been the model of peace and security we are all striving to give the next generation. But guess what? Their whole family is still close. They are all my friends on Facebook, and every couple of weeks, there's a picture of their kids—the next generation of bright-eyed blondes—together. Once in a while, I see the principal's daughters at a reunion or wedding. All four of the sisters talk about trips they are planning to take together and how they work alongside each other to take care of their old, cranky dad.

All these years later, as I try to understand what happened to them after Hurricane Alicia, I understand it was this: flexible, liquid grace flowing between all of them. My friends, the bright, blonde girls, had freedom to be themselves, even after a tragedy.

After they lost their home, the priorities in their family changed. Actually, the tragedy shook up their family and forced them to change. Now, everyone could breathe easily in that house. I felt it. The kids knew that disobedience might mean a sharp punishment, but it also meant total forgiveness. Complete reconciliation. A deep understanding they were each flawed—and forgiven.

As I'm writing this book about building a culture of grace for the next generation, I hope for these same agile relationships for my own kids. This is what flexibility and grace and moving forward together look like.

Do you know a family like this, which has had to forgive one another often? Think of what might be the secret ingredient in this family's recipe that has kept them close all these years. How did they play out being flawed and forgiven? Write about that here.

_____

_____

THE PROOF IS IN THE PROGRESS

Recently I visited my old friend, Cathi (the second sister), in her gorgeous home in Dallas. We talked about the crazy few months after Hurricane Alicia, when we found her Smurfs nightgown tangled in the weeds along the sand dunes. I asked her if she thought surviving such a catastrophe helped her deal with what life would eventually deal out.

She said, "Not just the hurricane. A lot of what my folks did helped us kids to be tough. Even buying a house on the beach—who moves their family there? But all our moving and readjusting taught us to take care of one another. We had to get along. You learn to care for your siblings."

What are the lessons here for our families? Put your kids through hard times? Give them lots of free time? Move a lot? Destroy your house?

No, but I think the forgiveness, the rebuilding, and even the conflict in the principal's house taught my friends a lot of their scrappy skills at moving forward, at accepting life on life's terms, on trusting God, at having low expectations.

Let's remember this as we look at the roles you play in your family. You and your siblings will shift and transform and morph and adjust. Don't resist the change, but learn from it.

See every development as a phase, a season, as temporary. Friction and failure are all going to happen. But the rebuilding can be the best part of your family. These changes allow you to learn about flexibility, forgiveness, and faith.

Let your family be like a feathery, light palm tree. Like palm trees, flexible families let the winds of grace blow through their branches. Accept the movement and the change the winds of life bring. When storms pass through your family, forgive one another. Keep coming back to the grace, to one another, to the love of family.

But, mostly, keep returning to the roots—to the love of your Savior—the one holding you all together anyway.

Are you teaching the next generation flexibility and forgiveness? What struggles has your family recently survived? How did you show grace to one another? How were you flexible? How did you rebuild?

_____

_____

_____

PALM TREES AND HURRICANES

Let's look closer at those palm trees. God created these trees as the perfect beach trees. Not only do their willowy fronds feather out in the strong seaside gusts, but their umbrella-like branches shield the beach (and beach bums) from the burning temperatures. God's design is incredible here. The bendiness of these regal trees is an excellent example of grace-based families.

If you've ever seen a hurricane, you've seen the coastal palms wave and sway in the one-hundred-mile-per-hour winds. These winds are like the hard times that blow through our families. Death. Disease. Arguments. Abandonment. Screaming fights.

Palm trees sway in all hurricane-force gusts, but they don't break. The streamer-like branches flitter. The trunk of the palm tree stands firm, and this is what agile families do when tragedy and change blow through their little tribes. Elastic families change roles, they forgive, they communicate, they treat one another with tenderness, they support the weakest branches. They identify problems and offer solutions. They show love and grace to one another.

This kind of transforming grace can only come from God. As humans, we're not this flexible on our own. Relationships need radical forgiveness, the kind of mercy that takes humbleness, repentance, and a sincere desire to get along better.

To be clear, this kind of transforming grace can be so hard and messy. As sinners, we resist it. If we were able to create better relationships on our own, if our human brains had figured out a way to orchestrate agile, well-adjusted families with some kind of pill or technology, we would all sign up for the easy way, the instant gratification way.

If the pill worked, none of us would agree to real transformation—for sanctification from the Holy Spirit—for authentic conversion.

It's the Holy Spirit that makes our families like those breeze-filled palm trees. It's the Spirit that inspires love, humility, patience, grace, and true kindness.

Still don't believe me? Let's look at the alternative, the different kind of tree.

Imagine if psychiatrists found a surefire prescription for guaranteed family harmony. The pharmaceutical company that created it would make a fortune. But why is God's way of learning lessons better than a quick prescription? Do you have a story about this kind of spiritual transformation, the kind that changes you? The kind that involves the fruits of the Spirit?

_____

_____

_____

_____

The Pastor, His Family, and Oak Trees

Back to Galveston, Texas, in the 1970s and '80s, and the pastor of our little church. This man was very German and strict. He jogged on Seawall Boulevard every morning before sunrise and drove a pragmatic Volkswagen, back when VWs were known as the car of the working people.

He was a rigid dad with a buzz cut and a deep baritone voice. He expected his sons to work hard and follow his rules perfectly. He also had very high expectations for his congregation. When one mom brought her baby to church and he squawked, the pastor stopped the sermon to ask her to take her baby to the nursery. I've never forgotten her look of shame when that poor mom ducked out of the sanctuary.

The pastor's wife, however, was not severe at all. She was like a beautiful fairy godmother that we kids adored. She was so tender and sweet-natured that she seemed fragile. On afternoons that my parents sent me to play at the pastor's house, I took mental notes about everything she did: Fresh daisies from the yard in a jelly jar. Red Kool-Aid in a real glass pitcher. Repainting the picket fence in front of their house every year.

The pastor's family lived in a tall yellow house on a street lined with ancient oaks in Galveston's historical district. Theirs was the kind of stoic, gorgeous home that was the perfect setting for festive holiday get-togethers.

Even in the tacky 1970s, our pastor's wife was the Jackie Kennedy of St. John's Lutheran Church: elegant, gentle, and classy. My gaggle of girlfriends—

including the principal's daughters—watched her with awe. To church pot-lucks, she would bring a tray of homemade marshmallows covered in dark chocolate. Who was this magnificent woman?

And, of course, we watched her sons. There were three of them—the old-est was two grades older than I was, the middle one was in my grade, and the youngest was in the grade behind me. At our tiny parochial school, my friends and I had a front row seat to watch the pastor's cute sons grow up.

They were a study in birth order—so stereotypical, it was if they were play-ing the roles in a movie. The oldest was fantastic at every sport, but he was especially talented at baseball. He would later go on to get a full scholarship to Notre Dame. Even though he was an overachiever in everything—and the successful darling of our small congregation—he was also mean. The nick-names he gave me as a child still sting ("Four-Eyed Punk" about my Coke-bot-tle glasses and "No-Comb" about my stringy hair).

In contrast, the middle son—the one in my grade—was a mess. His Trap-per Keeper was always dripping spelling tests and math assignments. He was constantly daydreaming and drawing. He was the most like his mom, so ten-der and sweet. He had a sense for how to make anyone feel special.

Finally, the baby of their family was the clown in every class. He was the funniest kid in our school, the one who recreated Saturday Night Live skits for our school's talent show. He changed the words of every hymn to something funny and slightly naughty. After school, while my mom graded papers in her classroom and his dad worked over at the church office, he would tell me sto-ries so hilarious that Steve Martin would have cried with laughter.

But he could also be so serious. During our afternoon chats, he told a different story about his family than who I thought they were. The house he was growing up in was a hard one for a kid. His dad yelled all the time, and his mom would close herself off in her room. Their house was filled with rules but no relationships.

Have you known a family of oak trees—one that relied on rigid rules and roles? What was your impression of a family like this? Or if this was your family, what was it like to live in a house with rules but no relationship?

HURRICANES AND OAK TREES

The pastor's family evacuated to their grandma's house in St. Louis for Hurricane Alicia in 1983. Their dad returned a few days later to find his family's beautiful, yellow historic house had flooded. It would take months to replace the hardwood floors.

The worst damage at the pastor's house was to the big oak trees. Salt water had soaked the roots of these majestic trees, and they had died from the poison. This happened to many of Galveston's oak trees after Alicia. Tree crews traveled up and down our historic streets—Postoffice, Church, and Winnie—cutting down dead oak trees and grinding up their stumps. Even after our pastor's yellow house had new floors, it was never the same. It looked undressed without the tree's leafy shadows dancing across it.

While our pastor managed the floor project and helped members of our congregation, his wife and sons stayed at their grandma's house and went to school in St. Louis for a couple of months. We missed them like crazy.

When our friends came back home, the boys told us horror stories of life at Grandma's. They said she was strict and weird and harsh. The youngest son, Erich, spun morbid, hilarious stories about life with their grandma.

After the hurricane, the pastor and his wife weren't the same to each other. Erich told terrible stories about the fights they had. His mom hadn't wanted to come back to Galveston after the hurricane. Even with their gorgeous house and her fancy parties, she was moody and lonely. She had frequent migraines (Erich later said it was actually depression) and spent many mornings in bed. This irritated her husband to the point that he gave her the silent treatment. She would often cry and threaten to take the boys back to her mom's house. Erich said the boys hid out when their parents fought. No one talked about it afterward.

Erich reported that their mom would disappear into herself, relying on the boys to step into their roles as The Boss, The Caretaker, and The Scapegoat. She would close herself off in her room for days. The oldest son would take over and bully the other boys into finishing their homework and chores. The middle son, the sweet one, sat in bed with his mom, watching endless TV. Erich was always in trouble, so he hid out at the neighbor's house to escape his mom's frequent hysteria and his dad's tirades.

Years later, this family has not yet found its footing. Erich reports his mom has turned into her own mother. The house she still shares with her pastor husband is like a museum. Erich doesn't visit much. He says it's still a place where "they tell you to take off your shoes but don't ask how you're doing. No one talks about anything. It's yelling or silence."

The oldest son became a doctor and married a woman whom Erich calls "frigid and rigid." The sensitive middle son has had a rough time. He's been married twice—once to a fun-loving drug addict he knew from high school, and now to an outspoken atheist. His parents disapprove of her and they are all at odds.

Try this: list five expectations that your parents had for you when you were growing up. Now, next to each expectation, write what happened if you didn't fulfill it. Did you receive an appropriate consequence? Were you forgiven? Did your parents hold you accountable? Did they make you feel guilty or ashamed? What did you learn from this?

OAK TREES DON'T BEND

I wonder if this family chose the stately yellow house—the one with the massive, foreboding oak trees—because the regal, rigid branches appealed to them. The old German pastor, with his love of strict rules that shouldn't bend, always called these trees "majestic."

His beautiful wife must have also liked the impression those big oaks gave. "We are a solid family. We are protected. Security lives here." Surely, on some level, this was the kind of family she wanted to raise. Maybe she didn't know that security and strength come from something much deeper than what a house looks like on the outside.

Rigid family oak trees don't serve us forever. They can be so grand, so gorgeous, that they do seem to promise structure and security. But these trees are also prone to catastrophic breaks. Isn't this the same for families that are too severe, that favor rigid roles, that resist flexibility and grace?

Yet, for many of us, our urge is to organize our families into these same unyielding roles, to never let them change. Families often fall apart because we can't adjust to changes, we can't bounce back after tragedies, we shun the elasticity that grace gives.

Our human hearts crave organization and absolutes because we hope they'll deliver security. We want to keep each person in his or her assigned position forever. You, sister, must be the caring, good listener who will help us all feel sensitive and connected. You, uncle, must be the one who earns lots of money and makes us look like a good family. Please, brother, don't change from being the messed-up one who is on the wrong track. You give me a reason to fix and help and feel needed.

When I talked to families about what has caused the worst conflict between them, so many said they didn't feel accepted by their families. Often this is based in a culture of fear. Their parents and siblings expected them to stay exactly the same forever, to play the same roles in the family. These friends confided that they weren't comfortable enough to be themselves. Adult siblings complained they couldn't relate to one another anymore.

Other friends talked about the pain of old fights. After family feuds, sisters said they never talked about what happened. They never forgave each other or felt forgiven. They didn't really believe the other sister had changed or that the fight wouldn't happen again. The infection of these old fights festered right beneath the bandages they had put over them.

These family members never considered the transformative work of the Holy Spirit. They never considered that a culture of grace allows our families to shift and change and transform. Instead, they clung to old rules, roles, and relationships.

Think about the roles you play in your family. Are you the Hero? The Princess? The Mess-up? Tell a short story about when you've demonstrated the characteristics of this role. Tell how you've changed from this role. Has your family embraced you as you've grown and matured?

_____

_____

THE STRANGE BREW OF YOU

You are so much more than just that role.

God didn't create you from some kind of a celestial Jell-O mold, specifically designed to fulfill only one position in your life. He doesn't have a Personality Conveyer Belt that cranks out human prototypes like an assembly line. Princess. Hero. Black Sheep. Sweetheart. Hostess.

Even if your family would like you to play one part forever, that isn't how growth and grace work. The roles of your childhood crumble; you rebuild your identity around who you've become. Conflict and tragedy blow through your life and you learn better skills. God changes your circumstances and then forms new skills in you to adapt. In a culture of grace, your family sees the good works happening in your life and supports who you are growing to be.

You are God's work in progress. You are becoming, and becoming, and becoming—through the hardest seasons that you have yet to discover, through delightful surprises from your Savior, through a new understanding of your Father and how He wired you.

God is the original Author, and He often takes a lifetime to tell the story of you. He created you to be a mystical brew of everything that He knitted in your mother's womb, plus the unique dot-to-dot of experiences He's given you, mixed in with sprinkles of strange and exciting interests and talents.

Most of all, you are a student of all life's teachers. Unfortunately, the instructors in your life have often been failure, disease, disappointment, and conflict. But your other teachers can also be the Holy Spirit, unconditional love, loyalty, friendship, and the example of Jesus Himself. God gave you all these experiences, and He will give you so many opportunities to learn about grace, mercy, love, and His sovereignty.

Yes, God assigned you to your family, but that's not the end of your story. He also gave you the many experiences that stretch you and show you the crazy-fun-challenging path He has laid out for you. Just look at the families in the Bible—or for that matter, any of God's people. Over and over, God took men and women who should fit into Mold A and then stuck them in Role Q.

What more can you ask for than this? As you grow as God's child, you realize that His design is intentional—you are wired a certain way and your parents have preset expectations. But throughout your life, you will grow and change and morph forever.

The best news? As His children, there's enough grace and love to carry you through the most extraordinary seasons.

No matter what, He will take care of you.

List ten words that describe you. Next to each quality, write how you show this characteristic in your family of origin. Do any of these qualities not work with your family? Why? How have these characteristics helped your family?

_____

_____

_____

_____

THE LIE OF ONE DIVINE PURPOSE

For years, since I was in high school, people have told me that God has a specific calling for me. Authors and pastors and evangelists have encouraged me to find my purpose—the one exact path that God created especially for me.

Maybe like me, you've bought into this idea. You've seen your life as a funnel toward your single, God-ordained calling. Our scared human hearts LOVE the promise that there is a solitary path for each of us. Of course we do. This is works-based righteousness at its best.

Work harder. Concentrate more to fully understand the bread trail God is leaving for you. Focus more on the signs. Figure out the role you're supposed to play. Try more.

If you don't know the next step, it's because you're not paying close enough attention. With enough effort, you will find the one note God needs you to play, and you will please Him by playing that forever. The world is depending on you, and only you, to fulfill this call for His kingdom. No wasting time. No going through a phase. No meandering. Find this one purpose God has for you and stick with it.

But no. This is a lie. This idea is based in a culture of fear, the idea that you are predestined, predetermined, and preorchestrated to play the one role that your family needs you to fill.

No room for you to be the Sensitive Daydreamer—that role has been filled, thankyouverymuch. Back away from the kitchen, we already have the Family Chef. No need to apply to be the Responsible One, that's clearly not you. We already have the Boss here, and it's definitely not you. Don't drop the ball on your divine assignment or everything will crumble!

Lies. Lies. Lies. God is not this linear. A cookie-cutting Creator who only has four molds did not design your life. God never tells us He has only one divine call for you—in your family of Christ or in your family of flesh or in His whole creation.

Instead, God gives us the Bible, with stories of men and women so real we can practically feel them breathing from the pages. These are people who have crazy, mixed-up lives. God's message through these men and women is "You Are Called to Me" . . . not "You Are Called to This Specific Job."

When have you believed the idea that you are called to one specific job, one particular personality, one way of life, one role in your family? What security did this give you? In what ways is this works-based righteousness?

_____

_____

_____

You Are a Stoner and Only Will Ever Be a Stoner

Look at Paul. At any particular time in his life, he could have declared himself to be on one mission for God—but what would that have eliminated from his life? What if Paul had listened to the ONE DIVINE CALLING nonsense and resisted God's growth and change?

For example, Paul could have believed, "I am Saul, the Pharisee, and only will ever be a Pharisee because this is God's specific call for my life. I am the one with enough fury to stone this Jesus lover, Stephen. Forever I will be the Great Stoner of Those Who Love Jesus. Amen."

Except, then the Road to Damascus happened. Suddenly, here is the actual, living, breathing Jesus standing in front of Saul. And just so Jesus gets his attention, He literally blinds Saul to all other options. Jesus says, "But rise and enter the city, and you will be told what you are to do" (Acts 9:6).

Did Paul feel like he hadn't been paying close enough attention? Did he think he had now discovered his true calling was to be the Blind Pharisee Who Can't Get Over His Horrible Sin—Forever? No. He did what he was told to do; he heeded this radically new calling. He started answering to the name Paul, and he used his zeal from his stoner days to travel to the worst heathen places on the planet.

What kind of faith did this take for Paul? To accept that THIS is his one and only divine purpose? But here we can see Paul living according to God's new calling, to be the Good News Spreader . . .

But then, prison!? Noooooo, God. Remember the Stoner Plan? Or the Pastor with All the Glory Plan? Paul is clearly not prison material. He's good at speaking, Lord. Didn't You create him to be the Prophet with the Big Message? Really, his one and only divine calling is to sing hymns in prison for the rest of his life?

Wait, God. Now You want him to be Long-Winded Letter Writer? But remember? He had just discovered Your Holy, Perfect, Specific Plan for him—again. Now You expect him to just become the Church Builder? But You engineered Paul for passion and drama, Lord. Where is that in letter-writing? Okay. As long Your perfect plan didn't create him to be some kind of a mentor to the next generation of pastors. Because he clearly doesn't have the patience for that.

Wait. WHAT?

Consider Paul's life. What was he committed to? How do you see this throughout the different seasons of his life? How did he have to be flexible? When has God asked you to be flexible? How have these different roles challenged you? How have they blessed you?

_____

_____

_____

_____

Vocation and the Vine

Martin Luther taught that as a Christian, you are called to specific vocations at different times throughout your life. This means that God places you in roles (sister, father, teacher, husband, pastor, accountant) for a bit or forever.

As your roles change, He equips you for this work. These tasks will most likely change and shift throughout your life. No single divine role, no solitary calling, no grand plan that your life must follow like a recipe.

In other words, Paul's Only Divine Call Forever and Ever wasn't to be a stoner. He was called to be a teacher, a preacher, a prophet, a mentor, a son, a brother in Christ, a disciple, a truth-teller, a prisoner, and a friend. Paul was not an oak tree; he was a swaying, bending palm tree, firmly planted in the soil of Jesus Christ and His promise to take care of him.

Martin Luther also lived a palm-tree life. His vocations were a similar Roller Coaster of All the Roles: Scholar, Monk, Reformer, Husband, Writer, Encourager, Preacher, Dad, King's Enemy, Rebel, Truth-Teller, Evangelist, Debater, Host, and Teacher. Like Paul, Luther was All the Things—the Boss, the Diligent Student, the Rebel-Rouser, the Cynic. God increased and adjusted his skills according to the specific tasks God laid out in his life. His life and his family were agile—they changed according to his new callings.

Paul writes in 2 Corinthians 5:17–20 that living as a new creation means you are an ambassador of Christ in whatever you do. Your calling is to spread the Good News, to live an obedient life in the roles where God puts you, to love others, and to love Jesus.

Oftentimes—most of the time—this looks completely opposite of a nicely organized life. A culture of grace often feels way more chaotic than a culture of control. As we say in our household, "Everything is a phase." This helps remind us to be flexible to the winds of change. This helps us remember that it's God who equips us for the seasons that unfold in our lives and in the lives of those we love. Really, it's such a fun way to live.

Our Lord is the very best kind of Father, not the kind that deals with us only if we stay in prescribed roles forever and ever. This is such better news than one note you must play forever and ever. He is the Life inside each and every one of us. His Holy Spirit is ever-changing, ever-equipping, ever-inspiring, ever-teaching, ever-sanctifying.

Could you learn to be this kind of earthly father or mother or sister or brother? Could you leave the past seasons behind and let grace grease your relationships? Could you trust that God will keep equipping you for each vocation He gives you? Could you embrace the work God is doing in the lives of your siblings and parents?

List ten vocations you have right now. Are you a son, a mother, a sister, a boss, a niece, a teacher, a husband? What past vocations have you had? What future vocations do you pray God will give you?

_____

_____

_____

_____

ROLE REVERSAL

I would bet the money you spent on this book that the career, spouse, and lifestyle you've chosen have everything to do with the role you played in your family.

If you were the responsible older child, you probably chose a profession managing other people. You're comfortable with everyone relying on you, and it feels so good to be the one in the room with the answers. Success is a narrow road for you, and you only feel like you've done a good job if you've been responsible. You are dependable and can't stand it when others don't follow through.

Except, you might also feel like all your value is tied up in your job. This is where your role on earth is not the same as it is in heaven. Because maybe God has a new vocation for you where you aren't the one with the answers. Maybe you're terrible at this new calling, and you have to learn entirely new skills.

Or perhaps, you're the silly, fun-loving, hilarious youngest child. Your family loves you because you can ratchet down everyone's stress. Your wife adores how you can help her relax. Your friends know they can count on you to make life more fun. But then God calls you to be the dad to a severely ill daughter, and you need to fight for her care.

This is what happened to my friend Erich, the youngest son in the pastor's family from 1970s Galveston. His daughter, Daisy, was born with cerebral palsy and needed more than fifteen surgeries in the first decade of her life.

Suddenly, Erich found himself on the front lines against doctors and insurance companies, advocating for more innovative treatments and better care for his sweet daughter. His skills to tell stories and make people laugh weren't so useful in this new role. But this was definitely the new vocation God was giving him. And the Lord was also giving him the faith, energy, insights, and right people to help him figure it out.

God changed my friend Erich through this experience. Gradually, he realized that he had a whole new set of skills. He left his career as a high school PE teacher and started working more and more with the care ministry at his church. Through this, he discovered he was good at walking alongside the very ill. In fact, he loved being able to help people with their deepest faith struggles—and not just by making them laugh.

Who knew?

Divide your life so far into at least five different seasons. Which roles has God asked you to play in these specific times of your life? What have you learned about yourself? What have you learned about your heavenly Father and how He equips you? How has your family reacted to your different roles?

_____

_____

_____

_____

BE A PALM TREE FAMILY

As Erich has tried to plug back in with his family of origin, it hasn't gone well. They already had a hero of the family, the oldest of the family, and everyone really needed to keep it that way. When he told his parents that he wouldn't be able to join them for his mom's annual Christmas party, they fought back.

Why not? He didn't come home last year either. They expected him to show up. No excuses.

On the phone that afternoon, Erich shared some of the struggles he and his wife were going through with Daisy's treatments. He expected support from his parents—instead they told him what he should be doing. They were full of advice and criticism. The call ended when Erich hung up, exasperated.

His mom and dad were probably scared. After all, if Erich's role was changing, what would happen to the rest of them? Their fear told them that his new demands were a betrayal to the family system. The salt water of crisis soaked their roots and poisoned their family tree. No wind could blow through these branches.

What could this family have learned from the principal's family? Or even from the palm trees down by the beach? Could they have seen themselves as those fluttering ribbon branches that dance gracefully in the winds? What kind of change of heart did they need? How could they have understood that grace and love move best through the agile and the flexible?

Is there some wisdom for your family in the way the fronds of a palm tree bend in the breeze? Could you see the deeper lesson here—that God's grace and the Holy Spirit are all dynamic, constantly changing, unbelievably creative, and exciting? Could this show you that it's okay—maybe even God-ordained—for your brother to move back in with your parents to save for law school? Could you trust that your dad really has changed, that he's ready for a new relationship?

Could those pliable palm tree branches remind you of Jesus' parables of paradoxes? He told stories that didn't turn out like anyone expected. He wanted the people (and you and me) to understand the creativity and flexibility and grace of a radical God who is with us every phase, every season, every breath of our lives.

Think of how Jesus' stories show agile relationships, full of radical mercy. The son who leaves home in rebellion is welcomed back as a prince. The enemy Samaritan is the one who helps the beaten and bleeding Jew. The responsible shepherd leaves the other ninety-nine sheep to go after only one. The stories in these lessons Jesus taught don't make any sense to our sinful nature. That's because they're about supernatural mercy. God's grace is extravagant and alive and revolutionary. These stories show a flexible faith and agile relationships.

It's this love—this grace—that's the most important part of any of our relationships, the most important part of our families. God shows us through the stories of the men and women He called.

And Jesus demonstrated it through the ultimate twist in His story. The King who lived a flawless life died as a sacrifice for us sinners.

This is the love that's at the heart of each of our lives, the grace that makes us God's children, that allows us to live faith-filled adventures, equipped with the Holy Spirit, sharing salt and light with the world.

Write the story about a recent time your family has been forced to act like a palm tree family. What turned your clan upside down? How did grace change the story? How do you see this happening with the next generation?

_____

_____

_____

_____

CONFLICT = COURAGE + FAITH

It seems to be ingrained in us to resist change. When one or more of us doesn't act according the prescribed human plan, there is always conflict. Why must the scary, different thing happen? THIS IS WHAT WE HAVE ALL BEEN AFRAID OF THE WHOLE TIME! NOOOOOO! But conflict and falling apart and change usually end up to be the very best for us.

Like other lifelong residents of the Gulf Coast, I've learned to dread hurricane season. When the meteorologists begin talking about "a storm brewing in the Gulf," we all tune our televisions, radios, Internet browsers, and Twitter feeds to What Might Happen. We panic, pray, and prepare for the worst.

Everyone starts talking about how this storm will be the biggest to ever "rip across Texas." We all plan what we will do after the Armageddon of the Storm of the Century hits. We stockpile water and plywood and evacuate to higher ground. No one can think beyond Landing Date because the uncertainty and destruction will be just too unbelievable.

Then, inevitably, the storm does strike the Gulf Coast and the one-hundred-mile-an-hour winds and the floods and destruction are the stuff that make international news. It's disastrous and terrible. Yes, this is absolutely what we were all afraid of. Entire shopping malls without roofs. Semitrucks turned over like Matchbox cars. Billions of dollars of damage. News teams crawling all over our community with the very worst stories. Recently, Hurricane Harvey dumped fifty inches of rain and caused trillions of dollars of damage across Texas and Louisiana.

After the destruction of the storm, harried survivors look into the camera and say, "We will never be the same. This city will never be the same."

These words sound harrowing. If a storm can demolish a city in one night, how safe are any of us? If complete destruction is just a natural disaster away, then what security do we have?

But here's what long-time islanders will tell you: hurricanes always bring change—for the better. That's right. These hurricanes rip off the old, crumbling roofs. They uproot the decaying trees and flood the eyesore, abandoned buildings. Afterward, the community has to come together to clean up the destruction, to pray, to help, and to rebuild. Neighbors help one another, and churches show up with repair teams and supplies.

After a hurricane, the history books show the disaster was beneficial for the city and its residents. Of course destruction is scary and inconvenient and NOT THE PLAN . . . but it always ends up being necessary.

Isn't this the way we always see conflict in our lives? We never have the courage for it on our own. We dread it and convince one another that the storm will be the end of everything safe and good.

But then the conflict dissipates, and the hard work follows, and the repair is where the miracles of grace happen. Don't you always discover that in your reconciliation, you can rebuild better than ever before? You learn that you never liked the old brown carpet anyway, and aren't these new hardwoods so much better? You learn that you had been in bad habits, and these new habits are so much healthier.

Yes, rebuilding relationships and homes is expensive and scary and totally inconvenient. But in times like these, you learn that God is the Provider. He takes care of the sparrows in the hurricane—and He takes care of you.

You learn that the old rules and the old *roles* were outdated anyway. You discover that you like your family much better when everyone feels free to breathe. You enjoy your parents a lot more when you can talk about the problems and the old secrets. You are much more peaceful when grace flows freely through your ever-changing, ever-growing family tree.

Has your family been through a storm? When? Write about it here. How did reconstruction help you to better communicate and to better show grace?

_____

_____

_____

_____

_____

The Oak Trees of Galveston and Hurricane Ike

One last tree metaphor because this one is so perfect to show what God can do through our families.

In 2008, Hurricane Ike, a Category 4 (out of 5) storm blew 145-mile-per-hour winds through Galveston. This was the worst hurricane to hit my beloved hometown in the previous one hundred years. The storm surge was devastating to the little island. Salt water flooded the roots of thousands of the city's trees, killing them instantly. Besides the more catastrophic damage, citizens were heartbroken at the loss of the community's treasured old oak trees.

Except . . . the dead trees weren't the end of the story. Where many saw ugly, lifeless trees, artists saw a chance for something new and beautiful, for rejuvenation. Several artists brought their saws and knives and created gorgeous sculptures from these old trees. Over several months, these artists breathed second life into the old oaks that once lined neighborhood streets and shaded homes (including my childhood pastor's old yellow house).

This reminds me of what Jesus did on the cross—and what God does in your lives and in your family. We see destruction . . . and He sees resurrection. We see end . . . and He sees beginning. We see the storm demolished—He sees it turned our trees into something more interesting. Something more beautiful. Something stronger.

Ask the Holy Spirit to help you show the unending grace of Jesus to those who need it. Pray this for your family, to welcome the winds of conflict into your lives. Pray, to bow and sway with them.

What other hopes do you have for your family tree? What more beautiful, stronger relationships are you praying will come from conflict right now? Write your prayer here.

_____

_____

_____

_____

Joy: An Olive Branch Story of Hope

Joy is my neighbor and also my friend. Over the years of living on neighboring cul-de-sacs, she's brought meals when we've gone through hard times and transported my kids more times than I can count.

Joy is funny and helpful and was literally elected Volunteer of the Year at our neighborhood elementary school. Her daughter, Sara, is our kids' favorite babysitter, and her son, Ibby, has enough personality for two kids. He also has Down Syndrome.

Joy's life changed completely in 2005 when she was living in New Orleans and Hurricane Katrina devastated the city. At the time, Ibby was a medically fragile newborn who had just come home from months in the NICU after struggling for his life at birth.

In a matter of a few months, Joy's life crashed and crumbled like the buildings in New Orleans. Hurricane Katrina not only flooded her home (they moved to Texas shortly after this), but it showed her a new way to think about life and to see God's protection. Joy would never be the same after Ibby's birth and Hurricane Katrina.

Because when it rains it pours (bad pun), this season in Joy's life was also when her father, who was in Florida, was sick. During her dad's severe illness, Joy was caring for tiny Ibby in New Orleans, who had been born at only thirty weeks.

At the same time that Joy's dad was slipping away from a lifetime of smoking and emphysema, Ibby was growing stronger. And just as the doctors determined that Ibby was breathing well enough to be taken off his ventilator, Joy's mom called with the news that her dad would also be taken off his ventilator. The doctors couldn't do anything else to save his life.

Before having children, Joy had always been able to be there when her family needed her. For years, she was a helpmate for her sister, Cathy, who has an intellectual disability and autism. But now, Joy couldn't be there to help the family navigate her dad's care or to rally with family around her dad's bedside. And, thankfully, Joy's older sister, Lori, stepped in and took up the slack for Joy.

"This was hard. My parents couldn't come to see Ibby, and we weren't sure what was going to happen to him. Also, my dad was slipping away, but I needed to be in Louisiana for Ibby and our daughter, Sara. Everything was changing so fast."

That shift in the family dynamic stuck. Joy's older sister, Lori, was the rock that supported their mother through the death of their father and helped transition her sister to a group home. Lori is now the one who visits Cathy often and checks in on their mother every morning.

Joy says that although the change has sometimes been painful and causes her guilt for taking a less active role in helping, she knows it's what she needs to do for now. Her dedication is to her family, to her husband, Richard, and to Sara and Ibby. She knows the time will come when she will have to become more involved with the care of her mother and Cathy, but she's thankful her family, especially Lori, understands that she is focused on her children while they are young and life in Florida is stable.

And Joy has a miracle to celebrate in her son, Ibby. "Everyone told us that Ibby wouldn't survive. We were planning his funeral. But when I saw what God can do and what He did do through the miracle of Ibby, I understood how He can do anything. And look at Ibby now—he will one day graduate from college."

Prodigal Siblings

My twin brother's name is Hudson, and we grew up arm's length away from each other—two peas in a pod. He was born twenty minutes after me, but he was the bigger twin. School was easier for him too. He has a really impressive photographic memory. I have the opposite of that. I need to read something about twelve times for it to make sense.

When we were in high school, he got involved with this group of guys on the football team. Rich jerks. That was the start. They went to parties and took these crazy trips. We wouldn't hear from Hudson for a couple days, and my mom would get so upset. Hudson didn't care, though. Everyone else was telling him yes.

In college, Hudson went to a big school and joined a fraternity, and they partied a lot. I mean *a lot*. These were tough years for my mom.

All that time I've been the good twin. I've watched Hudson and figured out the mistakes not to make.

Now what can I say? I'm living the life. I'm married, my wife is about to have our first baby, and I'm working at a job I love. He's struggling. Still borrowing money from my mom and blaming everyone.

It was so easy for him for so long that he didn't learn the lessons you're supposed to when you're young.

—Jacob, 34

And he said to him, "Son, you are always with me, and all that is mine is yours. It was fitting to celebrate and be glad, for this your brother was dead, and is alive; he was lost, and is found."
Luke 15:31–32

The Wild, Crazy, True Story of the Prodigal Son

The parable of the prodigal son is one of those Bible stories that shows true-to-life characters. But it also introduces us to this crazy, radical dad who acts the opposite of how he should.

And it's because of that dad that this is one of the most well-known narratives in the Bible. When you hear Jesus' parable about these two brothers, you can probably recognize the good son as a person in your own family. The older son might be very much like your perfectionist, judgmental older sister. You surely also know the black sheep son and his dramatic ups and downs because you probably have one just like him in your own family.

But the dad in Jesus' parable is something different. After his son ditches the family and comes back homeless and penniless, we expect this dad to have a long talk with him. We want the dad to lecture him about the importance of boundaries and responsibility. Also, it would be so nice if the dad could put his son on a payment plan for the money he blew on prostitutes.

The father doesn't do anything we want or expect, though. Instead, he does the opposite. Throwing this delinquent a party? Killing the prized calf? Who is this crazy dad, and what is Jesus' point in telling this story?

The point, as you've probably already learned, is to show us how extravagant God's grace is. And the parable is so radical because no one expects the dad's countercultural love, especially not the men and women crowded around Jesus the day He told the story.

In the crowd that day were tax collectors, prostitutes, religious do-gooders, and Pharisees. Did the prostitutes see themselves as the younger brother, as reckless sinners? Did the Pharisees understand that they were the older brothers, prideful and isolated? What did those original hearers learn about God that day? What did they think about this fictional culture of grace and the radical father who shared it with his sons?

Maybe like each of us, that original crowd recognized the family dynamics in Jesus' parable from what was happening in their own homes. These two brothers behave just like most of us do with our siblings.

The older brother is loyal to his family, but he's also locked in pride and conflict. He measures himself against his brother. He's figured out what his father wants and tries to do that well, so he can be successful. And the younger son swings from highs to lows with a rock star's drama. He seems both worthy of pity—and suspicion.

At the end of the parable, Jesus describes the kind of family fights we know from our own households. The older brother is frustrated because his dad doesn't see his loser brother accurately. He wants his dad to take his side. He wants to remain in his role as the savior of his family.

As we read in section 4, these are the kind of oak tree roles we can get stuck in forever. Because of our pride, we freeze one another out and ignore God's commands and examples of how to show grace to one another. On our own, we can never extend an olive branch of mercy to our siblings or parents.

We would rather live isolated and angry than risk a real, dynamic, changing relationship that's greased with grace. So, many of us live like this forever—never joining the party God throws for us. Never forgiving our reckless siblings. Never feeling fully forgiven.

So many of the men and women I talked to were living out the prodigal son story in their own families. Either they were like the younger brother (they had left their families and felt like they could never be fully accepted back), or like the older brother, they could not fully accept their reckless family members back into the family.

And still others felt like the dad in the parable, the one who extends the grace to both of his sons.

How is the prodigal son story playing itself out in your family right now? Have you felt like the lost family member, like the rebel? Or have you ever felt like the older sibling, the one who did everything right, who wanted to earn your parents' love? Write here which character you identify with the most. Why?

_____

_____

_____

_____

Lucy: The Prodigal Daughter

When I eat out with my friend Lucy, her dramatic looks always make people stare. She has a cute, small face; a long, lean body; and bright blue eyes. She also has the kind of haircut that usually only looks good on *Vogue* models—or Instagram It girls. It's shaved on the sides and platinum blonde and curly on the top. It's asymmetrical and beautiful and so interesting. Just like Lucy.

Our kids go to the same school, and over the years, we've become good friends. Lucy has had a complicated relationship with her family since she was little. Her dad is a successful trial attorney, the kind who defends oil tycoons and puts serious criminals in jail. I've met him a few times, and even for a grandpa, he's intimidating. He's more than six feet tall, with silver hair and the same sharp blue eyes Lucy has. Her mother is also interesting and intense, in the way that women married to powerful men usually are. Poised. Guarded. Striking. Patient. Wise.

Lucy grew up in a household where both her parents were very attentive (especially when it came to how Lucy was doing in school or soccer). They supplied everything Lucy needed to thrive: her mom volunteered at her private school; her dad was involved on every level of her life, from serving on the school board to helping her with her honors math homework.

"I was so loved," Lucy says about her childhood. "No matter what else happened after that, I can tell you that my parents took care of me so well. Every day they told me how much they loved me. The problems came later. The problems were with me."

Lucy says that she has always been too sensitive. She describes herself as the kind of child born with a "hole in my soul." From the time she was in elementary school, she felt too big, too self-conscious, too clumsy, too much of everything. She was as intense as her dad and as bright as her mom. But for Lucy, both of these traits made her aware of how she didn't fit in. Other kids could get over failing a spelling test or the argument with their mom. But not Lucy. If a teacher criticized her or she fought with a friend, Lucy would assault-eat a bag of donuts. Then, feeling sick, she would make herself throw up.

Lucy hated the way that her tummy poked out of her pink ballerina leotard. More than anything, she wanted to look like her mom, who was sleek and petite. By the time Lucy was in sixth grade, she was counting calories and exercising constantly. She liked the control it gave her over her body. Eating a whole bag of cookies and then throwing up was punishing her body. This felt right.

Also, the attention boys gave her felt right. By the time she was in high school, Lucy had a serious boyfriend who introduced her to pot. She reports that marijuana became her love then. "That's one infatuation that never let me down. That boyfriend cheated on me. And so did the next one. But weed was always there. It let me space out, take a vacation from my own brain. At fifteen, all I wanted was a vacation from my own brain."

Lucy hid all this from her family—she was even able to keep her grades up and still get into the National Honor Society. But secretly, she was a wreck. She went with her church youth group to the National Youth Gathering with a bottle of Vicodin hidden in her suitcase.

"I thought about suicide all the time. Anything stressful made me want to blow my brains out. I mean anything. Someone saying hi to me in the hall. Or someone not saying hi to me. Or—and this is the craziest part—when I had any kind of success. That was the worst. Because I always thought, 'It's such a lie. If this system will celebrate a mess-up like me, it's a bad system.'"

The one bright spot in Lucy's life was her little brother, Tommy. He was five years younger than she was and everything she wanted to be. Tommy didn't have the hole in his soul. He didn't need to escape all the time. Most of all, he could absorb all his parents' love and then shine it to the rest of the world. "Tommy has always been like a solar panel, he can store up good things and use them later."

One night, when Lucy thought she might be pregnant, she crept into her little brother's room and told him everything about her life. "He knew about the drugs and the sex. I even told him about the bulimia because he was so sweet and accepting. That night, I learned that Tommy could keep my secrets. I will always be grateful for that. Everyone needs a secret-keeper. Tommy was mine."

Perhaps the most comforting and confusing part of our relationships with our siblings is their intensity. Your brothers and sisters were your first friends, your deepest connection, your trusted confidants. Write about your experience with these first intense relationships here. Tell about a time of deep bonding between you and one of your siblings.

_____

_____

_____

_____

_____

THE TWO SIDES OF THE SIBLING RELATIONSHIP

Tommy was just starting high school when Lucy was graduating. By now, Lucy's relationship with her parents had deteriorated. They had found pills in her car, a pregnancy test in her bathroom, and she was failing more than one class. They fought often: Lucy refused to see the counselor they found her. She didn't believe in God. She had missed so much school that she was in danger of not graduating.

Even through these horrible years, Lucy's parents did what they could. They prayed and tried weekend trips with Lucy, away from her friends, so they could talk to her. They hoped that when she went to college and she left her boyfriend behind, she would rediscover her old interest in school. But Lucy's senior year was a new low.

Her grades had fallen, and she was accepted to only lackluster schools. Plus, she was so depressed, she had no interest in college. "My dad had made it his mission in life to find a college that worked for me. Except neither one of us could say the truth—that no school wanted a troublemaker like me. So I was a total brat about it. When my dad set up campus visits, I accused him of trying to control my life. We would yell at each other, and my mom drifted further from us, like she was an iceberg. Everyone was holding their breath, waiting for one of us to help the other. I hated my parents, and they weren't that crazy about me."

During this time, Tommy became more of everything that Lucy couldn't be. He was more of a scholar, more of a tennis superstar, more of a sweetheart—often hugging his mom or writing sweet notes to his dad after they had big fights with Lucy. Tommy always smiled, never argued about doing his homework or going to church, agreed to just about anything his parents or Lucy needed.

Lucy says that everything Tommy did made her life worse. She felt like she should be his protector, but she just couldn't be. Also, he was thriving in a structure that had failed her.

Most of all, she was jealous of him.

Sibling competition and sibling compassion determine how you understand the rest of your family and the rest of the world. What they are and what they are not will determine what you are and what you are not. Write how this was true for you.

_____

_____

_____

_____

"GIVE ME ALL YOUR MONEY"

Even though Lucy considers herself a prodigal daughter, she didn't leave her family as dramatically as the lost son in Jesus' parable did. She didn't demand her share of her family inheritance so she could go and have a good time.

Instead, she tried to commit suicide.

The summer before her freshman year of college, Lucy decided to do what she had wanted to for so many years. Faced with the reality of her recent abortion, and the fear she could never recover from that, Lucy carefully set out 100 aspirin on her family's mahogany dinner table. She started to swallow them one at a time, each with a shot of vodka. After every shot, she wrote a letter to someone in her family.

While Lucy slowly killed herself at the dinner table, her parents and Tommy were at his tennis tournament. They weren't scheduled to be back for hours.

But Tommy came home early. His parents had met friends for dinner after his last match, but he had left to get some rest before the next morning's competition. When Tommy walked through the door and saw Lucy passed out at the table, he called 911.

Even though the doctors were able to save her life that night, the incident had scarred her spirit forever. Lucy was so ashamed. She stopped talking to anyone, even her beloved little brother. Her parents were frantic. They enrolled her in the most reputable (and expensive) mental health hospital they could find. The best team of doctors and therapists in the country were working with Lucy to figure out if her pain was emotional or physical.

There were meetings and family therapy and prescriptions and talking and praying and trying to find what combination of all this would save Lucy. Her treatment cost thousands of dollars a day. Her parents gladly paid, so hopeful they would discover something to help her. They showed up every day, discussed and strategized, and kept praying.

Months later, when Lucy was released with the diagnosis of "highly anxious and severely depressed," she didn't have many options. The doctors advised her parents that a combination of support and independence would help Lucy launch a healthy life.

Her parents found her an apartment and got her a job as an aide at the church's preschool. Everything was strategized so Lucy could feel good about herself—and also so her parents could keep a close eye on her.

Lucy's parents tried to be patient, so she would see that she could be successful on her own. "The only problem, of course, was that I was really heavily medicated, scared, and my parents were funding everything. So I was like a ten-year-old. Or a very old person. I could handle nothing."

Lucy lived like this for four years, working with different therapists and taking baby steps in her relationship with her parents. They were all trying to figure out new roles, but the situation was nearly impossible. "My family's problem has always been that we are all too smart. We could look at one another and say, 'We are doing fine,' but all of us know the truth of what we're not saying. My parents hated it when I pointed out the truth. I would say, 'So this is pretty sad that I'm almost twenty-two, and I can't take care of myself because I'll end up back in the Mental Marriott.' My mom would just shake her head and tell me not to say that."

Meanwhile, Tommy was becoming more and more successful. Throughout his high school years, ever since Tommy had found his older sister that night, they had remained close. She counted on his cheerful reports from high school. He was in the same place she had been, with the same teachers and same pressures, but he made it all look so easy. Tommy's stories about class trips and youth group were like fairy tales to Lucy. Tommy had become her superhero, the one who could handle anything.

The one who had become what she never could.

Isn't it strange how two siblings can find such different truths in the same environment? Has this happened in your world? Write the story here. Which character were you—more like Lucy or more like Tommy? How has that difference changed your outlook?

_____

_____

_____

_____

_____

THE UNFORGIVABLE LIFE

Unlike Lucy, Tommy knew exactly what he wanted to do with his life. He loved his school's debate team, and he wanted to be a lawyer like his dad. The right universities not only opened their doors to him, but they offered him scholarships.

Lucy was starting to see her little brother wasn't just sweet and helpful and her personally-assigned guardian angel. She noticed that now that he was growing up, he wasn't always smiling. When Lucy watched him play tennis or compete in debates, she saw how bloodthirsty he could be. When he lost, he was moody and withdrawn.

More than once, he told Lucy about how he was choosing his college by the one that would give him the most scholarship money. Lucy said, "But mom and dad can afford college. They've been saving." Tommy looked at her like she was an idiot. "Not anymore. They've been paying for all this for you."

Lucy said after that—right around the time Tommy started school at Rice

(Texas's version of the Ivy League)—their relationship started to fray. Tommy became too busy to meet up with Lucy for coffee or dinner. She blamed herself. "I had been such a mess for so many years. Tommy started to see me as the screw-up I am. He had deserved so much more. He's such a good kid. But there are consequences for everything, and I had this coming from Tommy. He couldn't keep giving me a pass forever."

Lucy eventually found her own way. She became more involved in her church, learned healthy coping strategies for her anxiety, and she found an incredible support system of friends at the small Christian college where she started to take classes. Also, she met her boyfriend, Bo. He was the music minister at her church, who also helped with youth events. Lucy fell in love with his sense of humor and passion to help kids. By the time he and Lucy were serious enough to start talking about forever, Tommy was taking the LSAT and applying to law schools.

Even though Lucy and her parents finally got the genuine relationship they had prayed about for so long, she couldn't get Tommy to take her seriously or to spend time with her at all. Her parents invited her and Bo over for dinner almost every Friday night, but Tommy was never there.

When Lucy joked he was avoiding her, her parents wouldn't meet her eye. "I knew then that everything wasn't back to normal in our family. But, again, we didn't really talk about it."

Lucy took Tommy out to dinner and apologized for everything—for taking up so much of her parents' attention all those years, for the night of vodka and pills when Tommy had found her at the table, for all the money her parents had spent on her recovery. She cried and admitted that she couldn't ever repay everything she had taken from Tommy.

But Tommy wasn't interested in her apologies. Instead he told her, "It's hard for me to believe you're being sincere."

To Tommy, Lucy would always be a disaster.

Write about forgiveness in your oldest relationships. Is there something you did in your family years ago that you've never been forgiven for? Is there someone who hurt you long ago that you can't forgive? Write about that here.

_____

_____

_____

_____

EVERY HERO NEEDS A VILLAIN

Lucy knew how to feel ashamed, and for many years, she felt embarrassed when Tommy was around. He had accomplished everything that her parents had hoped for both of them. His grades had never slipped. He had never left God. And he had fallen in love with a woman as classy and competent as his own mom.

As Lucy marvels, "It's not fake with Tommy. He genuinely wants all those things. He's becoming a lawyer to help other people. He works hard to do his best. He makes the really hard parts of life look easy. We're like genetic mutations—he inherited all the good, easy parts of our parents. I seem to have gotten not enough—or maybe too much—of their strengths. I'm way too intense. I think too much. I feel everything so much. I always expect too much."

As Lucy and her parents learned to trust and enjoy one another again, as Lucy got married and found a job with a nonprofit that helps girls with body image struggles, she discovered a darker part of Tommy's love of hard work and doing the right thing.

She's come to understand that so much of his relationship with his parents is based on this, exactly. All those years, while Lucy had been lost, Tommy had enjoyed the status of the Golden Child. "He became like a counselor—or a savior—to my parents. When mom and dad were freaking out about me, Tommy got to be the one with all the answers. At school and at home, he was promoted to hero status. That messed with his idea of himself."

What Lucy has realized is that every hero needs a villain. So, even though Tommy had always been so sweet and supportive of her, he was also noting what *not* to do. Her absence, her failures, her hurts naturally carved out a space for Tommy to be present, to be successful, to be a healer. "From what my mom describes, those years that I was a disaster, Tommy did what any smart over-achiever would do—he worked hard to be Not Me. And that taught him some weird lessons about love. I think he started to believe my parents liked him because he didn't yell at them or smoke weed. He felt like he earned all their affection."

Now that Lucy is a fully accepted and functioning part of her family again, everyone is thrilled. Except Tommy. He's not ready to give up his role as the Good One. Like Lucy said, he has strong ideas about who deserves love.

All those years of perfect behavior had to count for something. If Lucy can come back after everything she did to her family, then what was the point of being so good all those years? Tommy's answer is that the family should still have a caste system—with him as the trusted, loved one and Lucy as the lower-class charity case.

"Bo and I have decided that the problem between Tommy and me is that he feels like he's out of a job. Of course he doesn't want me back for Sunday lunches. I'm the competition, and he likes to win. What I've tried to tell Tommy—what he'll never believe—is that I would have given anything to be like him. I will always be so embarrassed of the person I was all those years. They were a nightmare. I hate that I put my parents through all that."

A thorn in Lucy's recovery is that she can't make Tommy forgive her—or even like her. In coming back to her family, in finding her husband and her dream job, she lost her little brother. And he was the only thing she really thought she had.

But she wouldn't go back. "My parents and I went through hell. We really did. But all of it—my addictions and depression and anxiety and even the drugs and the abortion—taught me. Through all of this, I learned firsthand about the unconditional love of my parents and of my God. I learned about how deep grace goes. I hate to say this because it sounds mean, but Tommy doesn't know about grace like I do. I think Tommy believes you earn love by doing everything right." Here, Lucy laughs. "I did everything wrong—and through that I learned I'm loved."

What have you learned about unconditional love from your family? Have you experienced the truth that your family loves you in spite of what you've done? Or do you feel like they only love you because of what you can provide for them? Write your answer here. What's an example of why you believe this?

_____

_____

_____

_____

_____

THE GIFT OF UNDERSTANDING GRACE

What does Lucy's story—and Jesus' parable—mean for you today? You probably find yourself in one of the same roles as the two brothers in Jesus' story. The younger brother (the rebel, the scapegoat, the damaged one) and the older brother (the overachiever, the sweetheart, the good child) are a spectrum, and you fall closer to one end or the other.

Or, at different times in your life, you might find yourself on the opposite end of the spectrum than you were the year before.

As you can see in the parable (and by looking around in your own family), both of these roles experience blessings and burdens. The lost child struggles with so much heartache. This is the one who finds where the boundaries are by pushing on them. This is the child that learns lessons in jail cells and abortion clinics. But in a culture of grace, the reconciliation teaches the rebel about real love.

When the parents run to rescue the lost child, when he sees the hurt he's caused them and the love in their eyes, he truly understands what unconditional love looks like. Lucy knows grace is a free gift because she has seen that she deserves nothing else.

When Jesus told the parable of the lost son, He included this same moment of realization for the younger son. After the prodigal son has lost all his dad's money, he finds himself feeding pigs. He's so hungry that he considers eating the carob pods the pigs are eating. At that moment, the son fully understands his separation from his father. He says, "How many of my father's hired servants have more than enough bread, but I perish here with hunger! I will arise and go to my father, and I will say to him, 'Father, I have sinned against heaven and before you. I am no longer worthy to be called your son. Treat me as one of your hired servants'" (Luke 15:17–19).

Both the prostitutes and the Pharisees could agree with this statement. Yep. That is definitely a son who doesn't deserve his father's love. For Jesus' audience, this detail about the son's unworthiness sets up the next part of the story, the surprise climax. The grace.

Here's where those listening to Jesus' story couldn't imagine what was coming next: the father not only allows his son back into the household—he totally and fully accepts him back, not as a slave but as a member of the family. No, wait, even more astounding. He celebrates his son as a fully restored member of the family, like one who has been gone from home fighting for the family honor. The father does not treat the lost son like one who has been off wasting the family's money, time, and love. The father doesn't treat the son as he deserves.

This is, of course, the most important lesson for us in both our earthly families and our heavenly families. Whether or not we realize it, we are all the younger brother. Our sin and selfishness and self-absorption and humanness makes us the worst kind of mess-ups. We deserve death, treatment as a slave, only the carob pods of the pigs.

But God does the same crazy move as the dad in the parable. He runs for us, welcomes us home, kills the best food on the farm, and throws a raging party in our honor. He welcomes us into His family and His arms as His beloved child. We are snow-white, forgiven, and loved.

We are home.

Does this part of Jesus' parable, the total shame and unworthiness the son feels, make sense to you? Have you felt like an enemy of God? Or is the idea of that hard for you to understand or accept? How does this radical grace make you uneasy? How does it feel like good news?

_____

_____

_____

_____

_____

Love That's Earned

Or maybe you can't relate to this moment of grace at all. Perhaps this is because you have trouble seeing yourself as fully separated from God. To those of us who have always lived as the responsible one in our families, as the one everyone has celebrated as the hero, the idea of being the enemy of any father doesn't seem right. The moment of *dis*grace feels like something that belongs to other people. We haven't struggled with that kind of rebellion, so clearly Jesus' parable is for sinners.

The Pharisees in the crowd the day that Jesus told this parable definitely would have related to the older brother. They were the chosen people. Their ancestors were the ones in the desert, the descendants of Abraham. They had excelled at everything about God up until now. They had never messed around with prostitutes or bad ideas or wasted their family's time. They were the ones who had stood next to God, telling Him how disappointing everyone else was.

You and I can act like this too. When we feel like we're the superior ones in relationships, forgiveness doesn't really happen. For those who feel like they're benefactors, the idea of a merciful God is a watery idea, meant only to benefit *others* who struggle.

Except—and this is sooooooo annoying to the older brother types—each and every person has had lots of moments being completely lost. In fact, throughout our existence as God's sons and daughters, we are blind to just how sinful we are.

As a storyteller, I love the detail that Jesus includes about the older son at the end of His story. The older son, the one who doesn't understand grace, won't join the party. He's isolated, prideful, controlling, unrepentant, and hateful. He's not having a good time. He's the only one NOT part of the family right then. The son doesn't want to go to a stupid party with a flawed family that celebrates the wrong thing.

If there's one message that speaks to the hearts of Pharisees, it's that hard work yields results. Just like Tommy believed, you can earn anything and must earn everything. If a system is a good one, it rewards only hard work and good behavior.

But a Father who accepts any kind of sinner? Well, who wants to be part of a family like that anyway?

Many lifelong Christians appreciate the older brother's view. Is this you? Tell how you can understand how the loyal son would feel frustrated by the lost son coming home. Write down three ways you isolate yourself from those you believe don't deserve to be part of God's party.

_____

_____

_____

_____

IF YOU CAN'T UNDERSTAND GRACE . . .

So what's the answer? Does God want each of us to rebel and live as ungrateful, scoffing atheists for a while—just so we can fully appreciate being found, just so we can value our lives as Christians? Is there something sadistic about the father in the parable? Is he secretly rubbing his hands together, so glad that his wayward son will now have to fully appreciate him?

Those of us who struggle to understand grace might believe that. But, once again, we're missing the point. Jesus was telling the Pharisees and prostitutes that our humanness will always let us down. No matter if we see ourselves as deprived or not—we are.

We need God's adoption. We want to be at the party of eternal life. Because without God's acceptance, each and every one of us is living in the slop of the pigs, eating their carob pods.

For those of us who hope to pass down a better family portrait to the next generation, Jesus' parable extends to our actual families, not just our heavenly ones.

Again, we can see the roles we play in the flesh-and-blood brothers and sisters that we call family. When one sibling becomes a rebel, another feels he should become a savior. When one brother hurts, the sister sees the job opportunity for a healer. When the sister falls down at her job as loyal helpmate, the other sister will step up to save the day. Both children in the family will learn lessons from this: I am _un_worthy, or I am worthy because I work hard.

But it's the end of the parable, the end of our stories, when we learn the good truth that God's grace bats last. This is where we see that in grace-based families, one child is never more worthy than the other.

Children who live in a culture of grace know they cannot do enough good to earn the parents' love. Even better, they cannot do enough bad to lose it.

This is exactly the lesson we're trying to teach the world about Jesus, isn't it? You can never sin enough to make Him disown you. You can't work enough to earn eternal life. It's the good news of Christianity, but if we don't learn it in our flesh-and-blood families, it can be really hard to understand it in our heavenly ones.

What did you learn about unconditional love from your parents? Did they teach you that there was nothing too damaging you could do to lose their love? Did they also teach that there was nothing you could do earn their love? Write about these two lessons here. Perhaps include a memory of a time you learned one or the other.

_____

_____

_____

_____

THE TWO LOST SONS

To create a culture of grace in your home, it's important to understand which role you play and which your children might play. Let's take another look at the characters in your family and how each might struggle with grace—both feeling unworthy for it and feeling too worthy for it.

The family rebels will struggle with shame and fear of rejection. They struggle to move past their most reckless rebellion. The black sheep of the family find it hard to feel forgiven, always living in that disgraceful moment with the pigs, feeling unworthy and eyeing the carob pods. These children might not know how to reconnect with the family they hurt. They can't imagine full acceptance again. They feel like they will never deserve the prized calf.

The family heroes will struggle with pride. These children see themselves as the invaluable helpers in the family, the ones everyone looks to for answers. These children will understand love as a payment plan: I work hard and you reward me with acceptance. They will kick and punch against the idea of free grace. It will be hard for them to forgive the siblings they see as less worthy. These are the family members fighting against a culture of grace and arguing for a caste system.

Jesus tells us to love our brothers (and sisters) in Matthew 5:21–26, and this includes our literal, actual, flesh-and-blood siblings. And at the very heart of that love is grace. It's forgiveness.

Conditional love is not love—that's manipulation. It's self-serving. That might be how relationships often work, but Jesus' point in the parable is that it's not how they should work. Most definitely this is not the way our relationship with our heavenly Father works. He wants us to understand that our family/human/sinful ideas about love will always be flawed. But He is perfect. He is capable of only the kind of unconditional love we all want—it's the only kind He can give.

Fill in this blank: The love in my family is based on _____. What do you feel like you must do to be completely loved by your siblings? by your parents? by your extended family? What about your Heavenly Father? Is there something you feel like you must do for your Father to love you?

_____

_____

_____

_____

_____

REFLECTING UNCONDITIONAL LOVE IN FAMILIES

As we're trying to build a culture of grace in our family, I sometimes feel like we're building a culture of constant praise instead. In an attempt to avoid shame and guilt and to model unconditional love, I pour so many affirmations on my kids all day long. "You are so good for passing your spelling test!" "I am so proud of you for not hitting your sister back!" "You are my fantastic helper!"

I'm afraid all this achievement-based affection is training them to believe that they get all the love (praise, hugs, smiles, gratitude) when they follow the family plan for success.

We compliment our kids so much because we want them to understand that *this* is the right thing. Do more of this! Yes. This is good. Use your talents and show the love of Christ.

But in light of Jesus' parable, I'm afraid I might be training them to become works-based Pharisees. I often feel like I'm setting up a system the older brother would love. The point of Jesus' parable is grace, but I feel like I'm teaching my kids works-righteousness.

Of course, I'm not *trying* to do this. Our goal is to teach our kids self-control and discipline and how to be a part of a community.

We also discipline our kids when they don't study for a spelling test and when they hit back. Unconditional love looks like grace and forgiveness but also boundaries and discipline.

It's the father's words at the end of the parable that can guide parents about how to plant the seeds of a culture of grace in their households. To the older son, the father says, "Son, you are always with me, and all that is mine is yours. It was fitting to celebrate and be glad, for this your brother was dead, and is alive; he was lost, and is found" (Luke 15:31–32).

The father points back to the son's identity, his value because he has always been part of the family. In these last few words, the father restates grace in a few, short sentences and the important message: "all that is mine is yours." Because this is what it means to be a family together, belonging to one another.

Again, this is also the message of your dual citizenship. You are valuable because God has adopted you to be His child. Everything that He has is yours. This is what makes you valuable, not what you do or don't do. Not what you accomplish or don't accomplish.

What does unconditional love look like in your family? Write a letter to a family member you're struggling to show unconditional love. Dear _____, I love you all the time. I know we've struggled with . . .

_____

_____

_____

_____

_____

THE PERFECT FATHER'S LOVE

Is unconditional love the prescription in your family? Are you encouraging a culture of grace? Here are some questions to help you think through how your family functions:

- *What happens when someone messes up?* Is it common for your family to say "sorry"? Can you easily forget when someone in your family has hurt you? Do the adults apologize too? Can you remember a recent story when the parent in the family had to ask for forgiveness? How often do you talk about how you feel about one another, about your identity as family members? When someone in your family needs help, do they come to other family members? Do family members try to hide their mistakes from one another? When you talk about love with your family, do you talk about the things they do, or do you talk about who they are? (I love you, I'm so glad you're my son, you will always be my daughter.) What would happen in your family if a child rejected the family? How could you still extend grace to the lost child?

- *Most of all, do you believe in the unconditional love of your heavenly Father?* Do you talk about your identity as His children in your family? Do you talk about His forgiveness and go to church for regular confession and praise? Do you see yourselves as the salt and light of this love?

- *What about prayer?* Does your family come together to admit where you've messed up and to ask God for forgiveness? Do you also thank God for His forgiveness?

This love—the love of Christ—is the deep well of minerals where your family tree is planted. This love allows you to understand how to love others. It's Christ in you that keeps you rooted in your identity as a saved sinner. When you realize you're loved perfectly by your Father, you can understand how to freely share that love with your kids and extended family.

Here's a prayer you could try when you're struggling with a family member who is acting very unlovable: Heavenly Father, thank You for adopting me to be Your loved and saved child. Please forgive me for the times I struggle to act like Your child. Help me to forgive those who have hurt me. Help me to show Your perfect love to my family. Help me to be a picture of Your grace. Strengthen me to show Your unconditional love to my family, even those who reject it. Help me trust the work of Your Spirit. Heal our relationships, Lord, in Jesus' name. Amen.

Pray right now for your most difficult family relationship. Ask God to help you see that person as His beloved child. Ask Him to help you extend His grace to this person.

_____

_____

_____

_____

Seema: An Olive Branch Story of Hope

My friend Seema was raised in a progressive Hindu family. Growing up, she was raised to believe that enlightenment came through spiritual works. Her parents taught her that gods were in everything, around everything, and could be perceived as anything.

Spiritual enlightenment was found inside her own soul, through a place of relating to her own personal gods, in any way she wanted. Seema grew up completely sure of this. She truly believed that she was on the right path to becoming one with these gods.

Because Seema grew up as an immigrant, her family was tight-knit. Her family valued their beliefs and fiercely protected them and her from outsiders. But after Seema graduated from high school, she moved away to go to college. This was a move into a whole new world for Seema.

In Texas, Seema fell in love with freedom. She also fell in love with her now husband, Johnny. Right from the start, this country boy intrigued Seema. Johnny came from a small town and was deeply committed to his Christian faith. Their friendship was based on sharing their faiths with each other. It was through these conversations that Seema realized that she had been on the wrong path. True peace eluded her.

Johnny's deep convictions about his Christian faith caused Seema to question her Hindu faith. Eventually, over several months, Seema found herself drawn to Jesus and His message of free grace. Her new life in Christ began eighteen months after meeting Johnny.

Soon thereafter, Johnny and Seema married and started a family. Becoming a wife, and then a mother, was when Seema truly found herself trying to unlearn so much of her wrong beliefs about God. Instead of believing in millions of gods or seeking enlightenment in herself, she began to learn about the unconditional love of a heavenly Father.

I've known Seema for years, and she's constantly seeking God's Word, whether in church or Bible study, truly praying to understand God in beautiful new ways.

As you can imagine, Seema's transformation has been difficult for her Hindu parents. Seventeen years later, the pain of leaving her faith and rejecting her parents' beliefs still burns strong for Seema.

In many ways, to Seema's family, she is the prodigal daughter, who left her role as a loyal, rule-following oldest daughter to become a Christian. From her parents' view, Seema has rejected the most important part of the family's identity. She has turned her back on the belief system that knit them together. She has severed herself from the roots of her heritage.

Her parents feel like she has exchanged the Hindu path of enlightenment for a faith that tore their family apart. They have no understanding of the grace and forgiveness that Seema tells them about.

For Seema, the hardest part of becoming a Christian has been the struggle of loving her parents and sister well, while standing firm in rejecting their beliefs. For Seema's sister, the pangs of betrayal and rejection run deep, preventing them from truly knowing each other or forming a friendship. This is where the struggle is most difficult for Seema. How does she show grace to her Hindu family while remaining faithful and true to God?

Today, Seema has three gorgeous children who love God deeply. Her kids are such a beautiful picture of redemption, of new life, of an olive branch. Seema and Johnny earnestly strive to teach their kids to tell others about Jesus and His forgiveness—even their grandparents.

"For as long as I'm alive, as a daughter and a mother, I will continue to struggle with these relationships. Honoring and cherishing my parents while training my children to know they are loved by Jesus is a difficult struggle,"

Seema says.

Seema adds that parenting from abundance and love is so unnatural for her because she came from a faith-as-works upbringing. She will continue asking God for strength to show the kind of unconditional love to others that she has received from Him.

Most of all, she continues to pray that God will speak transforming grace to her unbelieving parents. This grace is the hope she holds onto dearly for her parents and sister.

She knows He'll continue to forgive her, to strengthen her, and teach her how to share His love with those who desperately need it. She will continue to rely on His strength and hope alone, so she, in turn, can love others.

Even the people in her family.

BETTER BOUNDARIES MAKE BETTER FAMILIES

My in-laws thrive on drama. My first several years in their family, I thought they just had bad luck. It took me about twenty years to realize they create most of their own problems.

A few years ago, my mother-in-law went through a health crisis with uterine cancer, and this was the very worst tragedy ever. I can't tell you how many conversations I sat through while she complained and worried—even though the cancer was highly treatable and she had all the best care.

Throughout every step of her treatment, she was hysterical about something. The doctor was the WORST insensitive idiot she had ever met. The nurses reported my mother-in-law had recovered the BEST considering the HORRIBLE tumor they had found. Through every step, she felt like she was DYING. Cancer is terrible. I get that. But my mother-in-law seemed determined to make it harder. It was important we all agreed that she had it the HARDEST.

It was during this saga that I finally realized the common denominator in all my mother-in-law's drama was herself. This became especially obvious when a dear friend was quietly dealing with stage III breast cancer at the same time. My mother-in-law could rant for twenty minutes about how her church family hadn't done anything to help her. At the same time, my breast cancer friend could go through a grueling radiation treatment and calmly report everything she was thankful for.

So I've had to learn to cut off my mother-in-law when she starts complaining. I don't have the time or energy to hear about her catastrophes. I was always afraid to do this because I believed that not listening would make her not like me. Which is pretty much what's happened. But I think she's found other people who will to listen to her rant. Now I can use my energy on real drama. Like my friend with breast cancer.

—Misty, 50

Humble yourselves, therefore, under the mighty hand of God so that at the proper time He may exalt you, casting all your anxieties on Him, because He cares for you. *1 Peter 5:6–7*

Where Are We on Boundaries: Yes or No?

Christian culture swings back and forth on boundaries. Every few months, a new blog or online sermon goes viral and announces, "This Is the Official Bible Stance on Christian Boundaries." "Listen up, Christians!" the tweets proclaim. "We have to have stricter boundaries in our relationships. Let your no be no."

But, then, a few months later, the pendulum swings, "Let's love like Jesus loved, with open hearts to everyone. Give the world full access to your time, your energy, and your love. Give them your cell phone number. Do anything for anyone!"

The concept of boundaries has flipped or flopped so many times that it's clear the issue is filled with questions and maybes. (In other words, the topic doesn't have clear boundaries—ha!)

Really, the flipping and flopping isn't unusual. We sinful Christians will struggle with the "right" way to act when it comes to deep, complex relationship questions. This is where our law-loving hearts crave strict rules. We like sermons like, "Make These Three Simple Changes to Discover Deep Peace, Respect, and Love." For these same reasons, it would be incredibly convenient if the Bible could be rewritten in tweet-sized bits of wisdom.

Our desire for quick changes is insatiable. This is why, every couple of months, a little wisdom quake about boundaries will make its way through churches. A book comes out that proves once and for all that we all need better boundaries.

Give your best yes. "No" is a complete sentence. Everyone has been abusing you with their ridiculous demands of your time and attention. Don't let your husband/kids/boss/parents take advantage of you anymore. They are asking too much of you. Flee from them. Establish firmer boundaries—for everyone from the barista who talks too much to your needy sister who is going through an ugly divorce. You are in control, and if you find your relationships are complicated, it's your own fault. Get it together, God's people. Perfect Christian harmony is just a better NO! away.

Then, a few months later, comes another book/article/blog/sermon series on the topic. No . . . wait! We are the Body of Christ, and this means we help one another. Be more vulnerable. You need more community and whole-hearted living. Gather around the table and break bread together because this is where true ministry happens. We are the hands and the feet of Jesus, and if you know someone who is hurting, it is your Christian duty to walk through that season with her.

Love is a verb—and that means showing up and living shoulder-to-shoulder with those hurting the most.

Right now.

Think about your relationship boundaries. As a Christian, do you feel like God wants us to have strict boundaries in our relationships, or does Jesus' example show we should be indulgent, passive, and always accommodating? On which side of the discussion do you fall? Write a couple of sentences about that here.

_____

_____

_____

_____

The Answer is a Definite Maybe

Clearly, the question "What kinds of boundaries should we show as Christians?" is complicated, with much gray in the answer. As anyone older than twelve has already discovered, most of life does not fit nicely onto Instagram memes. Sometimes, you have to tell your chatty aunt that you don't have time for a phone call. Sometimes, you have to wall off your brother because he has the power to shame you whenever he wants.

Then, other times, your uncle needs lots of your time helping him get a job at your company, and you feel like you need to help him. It's time to move your mom into assisted living, and it's a season of yes, yes, yes.

Boundaries are a complicated dance for which you don't know the steps. It's an irregular rhythm of dancing in the light, then stepping into the shadows, then light, light, light. Then more shadows. Then repeat. Anyone who tells you differently, any sermon or book or blog or person who gives you relationship advice that's a simple pattern of 1, 2, 3, is oversimplifying relationships.

Rules aren't at the heart of relationships, love is. As you've probably discovered, right below every *absolutely* and *definitely* and *all the time* waits the deep, murky water of *except, what about, sometimes,* and *maybe.* This is the cloudy space of unanswerable questions, complicated family dynamics, and sinful selfishness.

So, even though our human nature loves absolutes, when it comes to how to love others, we have to be careful of anyone offering one-size-fits-all advice for human hearts. You can be sure that once you learn it's right to say yes to everyone—you'll go through a new season where you need to say no.

But there is one answer when it comes to boundaries, and this is the one we'll look at it in this section. As you make decisions about saying yes and no, remember that it's God who cares best for His people. To understand how He does this, stay rooted in His Word. This is where you will find the constant guidance you need.

As you marinate in Scripture, God tenderizes your heart. It's here that you learn the good news that relationships are really, always and forever, unequivocally, about olive branches. Our God, who is powerful enough to create olive branches in your family, is also loving enough to care for every person's soul individually.

Think about a time when you've been sick or overcommitted and you've had to practice saying no. Think about different seasons in your life. Write about a season when you've had to learn to set stricter boundaries with others. What about a time when God has placed people in your life who needed a lot of your yeses? Which has been more of a struggle for you? Why do you think this is?

What Would Jesus Do (No, Really, What Did He Do?)

The bad news (or, perhaps, the good news) is that we can use Scripture to support the "you must have ironclad, no-compromise boundaries" standpoint. But we can also find plenty of Bible verses that support the "love everyone all the time" view. God's Word can be both a big yes to everyone in your life—and a big no.

Even Jesus—our gold standard, perfect model for human behavior—seemed to live a life of contradictions. Jesus loved the sinners and showed up around the dinner tables of everyone. He connected with both the tax collectors and the religious do-gooders.

We see Him turning water into wine at a wedding at His mother's request (see John 2:1–11). If you tried to turn this part of Jesus' ministry into a meme, the text would celebrate loose boundaries, something like, "What would Jesus do? He would show up and transform the party for His family! Because ANYTHING for family!"

Except Jesus didn't do this all the time. At other times, He told everyone He needed a break. Sometimes, He left a spiritually hungry, physically hungry crowd and went off by Himself to pray (Luke 5:16). This is the basis for those "guard your time and energy from those who would suck it all out of you!" sermons. The meme for this Facebook post would be a picture of Jesus sitting solo in a boat, in the middle of a lake, with a crowd of women holding children and men with leprosy gazing out at Him. The text on this one would say something like, "When the maddening crowd wants you to be everything to everyone, escape by yourself."

When we look at Jesus' relationships, we can find more inconsistencies. We see that He gave more of Himself to certain disciples, to His closest friends, Peter, James, and John (see Luke 8:51–52 and Mark 9:2–3). But He also left them and took a long walk by Himself when He needed time with His Father. He commanded His followers to baptize nations of people (see Matthew 28:19), but He also warned the baptizers to brush the dirt off their sandals if no one was listening (see Matthew 10:14).

We can even look at the way that Jesus treated His mom and brothers—

His own family—to find inconsistencies. He preached that we should love our families. He showed tender and responsible love to His mom, even while dying on the cross. He assigned His trusted friend, John, to take care of her (see John 19:26–27).

But He also told His mom and brothers to back off when they said they were afraid His ministry was too risky. He set Himself apart from His family with a strict boundary by telling them that now His disciples were His brothers and sisters (see Matthew 12:46–50).

The only story we have of Jesus' childhood is one of some pretty ruthless boundaries. The story of twelve-year-old Jesus staying behind in the temple always worries my mama heart.

It worried Mary's heart too. When she discovered that Jesus had stayed behind in Jerusalem to teach in the temple, she was (understandably) frantic. But Jesus reprimanded her for this and established a clear boundary: "Didn't you know I have heavenly work to do?" (see Luke 2:41–52).

What tweet-sized lesson can we learn from this? How can we create a list of "The Three Hard and Fast Relationship Rules for Your Most Difficult Family Members" if even Jesus kept changing them?

But there is so much good news in Jesus' example for us! God sent His Son to earth as an actual human, and because of this, we can see how He acted in relationships with actual people, how he loved and cared for each of them (a little of this, a lot of that, some more of this).

To understand how complicated relationships and boundaries and boundaries within family relationships can be, think about these examples from Jesus' life. What strikes you as inconsistent in the way He treated people? What can you learn from this for your relationships?

_____

_____

_____

_____

_____

Again with the Dual Citizenship!

If we can't follow hard-and-fast rules for boundaries in our relationships, we can lean on biblical principles. Jesus said these are the two most important principles in the whole Bible: Love God. Love others (see Mark 12:30–31).

This sounds very much like our discussion about dual citizenship: you are first a child of God, and you are second a child of your earthly family. This means that sometimes, because of your citizenship in heaven, you have to establish boundaries with your earthly family. If you need time with your heavenly Father, you might have to tell your earthly father that you can't help in his garden. When you need to rest in God's Word, it can mean that you don't have a lot of extra time to live as the super-helpful, productive child of your earthly mom.

Everything you do with your actual flesh-and-blood family here on earth should be considered as an extension of your spiritual identity as God's child. God is your ultimate authority about how to live as His child. You answer to *Him* about how you take care of the body and soul He gave you or how you're allowing other relationships to lure you away from Him.

Love Him and take care of His creation in you (your body, your time, your spirit, your habits, your life). After all, when God gave us the Ten Commandments, He absolutely acknowledged that the Christian life needs firm boundaries. Living as a child in the kingdom of God means you will have to say no to the person who causes you to gossip. You will need to rest and keep the Sabbath. And many times, you'll have to ask for God's help when a person becomes so important that she replaces God's role in your life.

As far as being part of our earthly families and loving them, let's look closely at how healthy boundaries can improve your relationships. In this section, we'll put your relationships under the microscope and talk about how saying no can not only clear up misunderstandings, but can also help other people to help themselves.

Remember that the deepest, best guiding principle when it comes to human boundaries is this: you are not completely responsible for any other person's health or happiness. God is. He loves everyone, and He can take care of His children the very best. Sometimes, He cares for His people through you; sometimes not.

Write about one relationship in which you have served as the primary caretaker for another person. How does it feel to be completely responsible for another person? What fear comes with this? Write a couple of sentences about what a relief it is that God is the ultimate Caretaker for all of our bodies and souls.

_____

_____

_____

_____

_____

Weird Family Politics and $25,000

Years ago, I worked with a wonderfully sarcastic, friendly, and wise person named Mandi. We taught together at the University of Houston as adjunct professors for a couple of years. We bonded over wry observations about our students—and the university's crazy strict policy for visiting professors' use of the copy machine. (We were given an allotted card for a maximum of 100 copies a semester. How, we wondered, could this be feasible? Only 100 copies?!)

Mandi was another Christian in this diverse religious and cultural environment, and we discussed the Bible a lot. We tried to answer questions about how God wants us to help the poor and how to treat our families. At the time, we were both freshly married and trying to navigate our new roles as wives and daughters-in-law.

Mandi also had a strange relationship with one particular family member, her great-aunt Mary, her grandma's sister. Although Mandi's grandma had been a wonderful Christian woman, Aunt Mary was not very kind. She was a widow without any children of her own, and she was bossy, closed-minded, a little racist, and very controlling. To complicate the relationship even more, Aunt Mary gave Mandi a check for $25,000 every December.

I met Mandi when we were in our twenties, and back then, the old, mean aunt and the $25,000 all seemed funny. Mandi would give weekly reports about this comically mean widow and the paradox of her extravagant gift.

Aunt Mary was the source of so many ridiculous stories—and she was also the source of much envy from the rest of us. Thanks to the yearly gift, Mandi bought a townhouse while the rest of us still had to rent. Then, the next year she used the money for what we called the Aunt Mary Memorial Kitchen Remodel.

Her aunt Mary hadn't actually died, but because we were young and insensitive, we had more than one conversation when Mandi admitted she kind of hoped she would. Aunt Mary had inherited millions of dollars from her late husband, and Mandi assumed that most of the money would go to her. She needed only to stay polite to her aunt and, eventually, she would be set for life.

The problem with that plan was that Aunt Mary really could be so cruel. She always commented on Mandi's weight. When dear Mandi was diagnosed with Type 2 diabetes, Aunt Mary looked at her (while smoking), and lectured her about "taking care of yourself." Her rant included the nutritional benefits of eating a daily lunch of Ritz crackers and canned tuna.

According to Mandi's reports, Aunt Mary felt free to say whatever she wanted. Her favorite conversations included her extreme views on what should happen to illegal immigrants, her distaste for the poor, her intolerance for slow grocery store clerks, mothers whose kids misbehaved in church, and waiters who delivered the wrong food.

After Mandi and I both had kids, I stopped teaching, but we stayed in touch over a monthly lunch together. Over the years, Mandi's time and patience for Aunt Mary began to wane. Aunt Mary had never liked children, so she preferred that Mandi visit her without her family. So what used to be merely tedious afternoons at Aunt Mary's house had now become almost impossible. Mandi had become a full-time professor (with full copy machine rights!), and she no longer wanted to leave her husband and kids to sneak away to Aunt Mary's dark, smoky house.

But there was the issue of the checks. Her aunt's money had given her family so much. That original townhouse Mandi had bought years ago? When she finally sold it, the value had tripled, and her family was able to buy their forever home. Plus, Mandi's kids had been in a Christian school for years, all thanks to the help from Aunt Mary. Mandi felt like the long afternoons with her aunt (*and* accepting the woman's long stream of criticism and anger) were the least she could do. Her time and patience were payment for the yearly windfalls of money.

Have you had a similar situation in your family? Write about a relationship where money has clouded your boundaries. Specifically, write a couple sentences about what guilt or obligation came with this relationship.

_____

_____

_____

_____

STOP THE MADNESS (. . . AND THE MONEY?)

But what to do? Mandi and I saw each other every few months, and she always had a long list of complaints about how the Aunt Mary situation was growing worse. The relationship was clearly troubling to Mandi because she talked about it more than she talked about anything else.

As Mandi's friend, the solution was obvious to me: Stop going to her house. You have to quit volunteering to show up and hear how your pants don't fit right. No, I don't want to keep your kids so you can spend your afternoon receiving more Aunt Abuse. Even if the $25,000 is now a necessary part of your budget, this isn't worth it!

At a birthday party for one of Mandi's daughters, I finally met the legendary Aunt Mary and understood right away that Mandi hadn't been exaggerating about her nastiness. Not only did this woman light up a Camel at this four-year-old's party, but she also stood over Mandi's husband, Keith, and loudly instructed him how to carve the brisket. Mandi flitted around her aunt, bringing her iced tea and cake and generally letting her act like a spoiled kid.

The especially strange part of all this was that Mandi wasn't a wimp in any other area of her life. Over the years, she had become known as a tough but fair professor. With four of her friends from her church, she had helped to establish a halfway house for pregnant teens. Mandi had single-handedly gathered donations for the charity, and they had bought a house, hired a full-time social worker, and now paid for the girls' doctor appointments. Mandi had even helped some of these women escape abusive relationships.

Why, then, couldn't she see that her Aunt Mary was abusive?

How can the strange ties of family (approval, money, love) bind us? Write about someone you know who is bound and blinded in a family relationship. How does this confuse boundaries for this person? What toll does this take? Has this ever happened to you?

_____

_____

_____

_____

A Line in the Sand/A Crack in the Relationship

Last year, Mandi finally stood up to her aunt. It happened one Saturday morning when Aunt Mary wanted to have two friends over for coffee. She asked Mandi to come over and help serve them. Aunt Mary had scheduled the little party months before the actual date. And then, of course, the day turned out to be the same morning as Mandi's youngest son's first Little League game. Mandi tried to talk to Aunt Mary about changing the schedule. She even offered to hire help for the morning. But Aunt Mary wouldn't even consider those options.

On the morning of the coffee, Mandi was angry and resentful that she had to be at her aunt's house rather than showing up for her boy. During the third hour of the morning coffee, Mandi couldn't stand it anymore. She was disgusted with her aunt's gossip, the way she barked at everyone, and her complete disregard for Mandi's schedule. She told Aunt Mary that she wanted to see her son's game, picked up her car keys, and walked out the door. Twenty minutes later, while Mandi was just getting to the ballgame, her cell phone rang.

As soon as she picked it up, Aunt Mary started to berate her for leaving, for embarrassing her, for acting so selfishly. But then Mandi finally told Aunt Mary that she couldn't take time away from her family anymore. She said, "I'm sorry, but I don't feel like you respect me. Our relationship has become too much."

Aunt Mary reacted to this just about like Mandi expected she would. She called her terrible names—ones so bad that Mandi had to hold her phone away from her ear. Then, when she realized that the other parents in the stands could hear what her aunt was screaming, Mandi hung up. Right away, a wave of relief rushed over her. Finally free and giddy from the liberation, she cheered on her son, who had just stepped up to bat.

When we talked about all this later, Mandi reported that she now felt guilty about the fight. Maybe she should have stayed to finish out the party—it only would've been a couple of hours. Also, she was very scared about (almost certainly) losing the yearly check and eventual inheritance that her family was counting on.

And finally, Mandi was surprised to discover she was sad that her aunt was mad at her. Even if the relationship had been overall bad, there were also some good parts. She liked to hear Aunt Mary's stories about her grandma; Mary was the only living member of that generation. Mandi started to worry that cutting off her aunt meant losing touch with that part of her family tree. What had she done?

She wrote Aunt Mary a long letter explaining that she missed her and that she hoped they could find a better way to spend time together. She also said that she was sorry, but she didn't feel comfortable with where their relationship was right now, and she could no longer tolerate the way that she spoke to her. Also, now that her kids were older, she wanted to bring them with her for visits.

At the family Thanksgiving get-together at Mandi's mom's house, it was clear that Aunt Mary had received the letter—and that she was furious about it. She made rude comments within Mandi's earshot about "ungratefulness" and "those who are only concerned about themselves."

But Mandi felt strangely free from her aunt's insults. She was able to laugh with her family—and even eat two pieces of pumpkin pie, despite Aunt Mary's glares. For the first Thanksgiving of her life, Mandi didn't care about the glares. Even though she was sad about the state of the relationship, standing up to her aunt had also diminished the woman's power in Mandi's life. Now she saw her as a "lonely old woman, who was used to everything happening on her schedule. No one had ever told her it couldn't. She bossed me around because I let her."

Then, that December, Mandi was stunned to open her mailbox and find the usual $25,000 check in an envelope from her aunt. There was no letter of explanation, so Mandi called her. Although Aunt Mary hadn't had a personality transplant or Road-to-Damascus moment, she was much warmer. She even thanked Mandi for taking the money. She said she was glad she could still help Mandi's family. This was another realization for my friend. Here, she had always believed that she was earning the money by being spineless and complacent. But Aunt Mary didn't see it that way at all. To her, sharing her wealth was an act of joy, completely independent of what Mandi did. She was dumbfounded.

Aunt Mary died a few months ago, and most of her money went to her church. This end to the story was actually a relief for Mandi. "I think all those checks, for all those years, were really confusing because I felt like Aunt Mary was taking care of me and I was taking care of her. When I 'broke up' with her, I realized that I couldn't make her happy. And she never wanted to make me happy. The check had been a whole separate thing for her. Giving to me was like giving to her church, I think. It was responsibility to God or family, but it wasn't related to my visits. Those were something else. I think she always believed she was really helping me with all her advice and stories. I guess because I never told her that she wasn't."

Now, Mandi says that she should have stood up to Aunt Mary long ago. Not only would it have been a much-needed relief to Mandi and her family, it would have helped Aunt Mary. She needed someone to tell her the effect her gossip and smoking and criticism and rants had on the people around her. Maybe she wouldn't have liked hearing this, but it would have been much better for both of them.

Write about boundaries as circles of responsibility. Draw a circle and write inside it what you are truly responsible to take care of, those people and projects that God has specifically assigned to you. Now draw circles for other members of your extended family. Write their responsibilities inside their circles. Are you responsible for the happiness of anyone in your family? Who, ultimately, takes care of them? How?

_____

_____

_____

_____

WALK AWAY WITH JESUS

My friend Caroline works as a women's ministry leader in a large church, and she has a saying for family members who have unhealthy boundaries or who push them to have loose boundaries: "Sometimes you have to let them walk away with Jesus."

This bit of advice holds so much wisdom. In every close relationship, there usually comes a time when it's necessary to redefine your circle of responsibility. This can be so painful that most of us are afraid to do it at all.

At the heart of this fear is the idea that you're shirking the duty that you have to make another person happy. The idea that another person's happiness is your job is a lie. You cannot change anyone else's mood or joy level any more than you can take away your mom's cancer or your brother's tendency to lie. None of us has that kind of control in this world. We most especially don't have that kind of control over another person's body or soul.

But God does. Only God does, in fact. This is the great news of relationships. We're not responsible for transforming other people. But transformation is God's greatest desire for His people. He can change anything about your atheist uncle or your cousin who isn't speaking to the family. These people can be flexible to the work of the Holy Spirit, or they can resist it. But it's up to them. Not you.

This means that the health, wealth, happiness, faith, and future of every person in your family falls squarely in his or her own circle of responsibility. You can pray for these other people—and you can let them walk away with Jesus. That is, you can trust that God is moving in their lives and taking care of them in ways you can't understand.

To be clear, this is some of the hardest advice to take to heart. If you struggle to watch your family face their own problems, you are so not alone. Defining stricter boundaries with a sibling, an adult child, or a parent can feel so wrong. When you believe the lie that their happiness belongs under your circle of responsibility, letting them walk away with Jesus can be almost impossible.

Pray for this person, yes. Show up with chicken soup and prayers, and love him or her with your hands and feet and whole heart. But also realize that you can only do as much as you can do. In the end, this person belongs to Jesus. You are responsible for your own faith. You're responsible for caring for children who can't yet care for themselves. You're responsible for your own wealth, property, and health. If trying to change another person's soul means neglecting your own, you've lost the boundary.

Mandi had to do this when her relationship with Aunt Mary damaged her ability to take care of her own family. Mandi avoided putting up a boundary ("I want to visit, but I need to bring my kids. Also, I don't want you to discuss my weight. I don't want you to insult other races in front of me or gossip or smoke in front of my kids. Please understand I can't make it this Saturday because our family has another commitment.") because she thought being spineless was helping her aunt. She was assuming her aunt's circle of responsibility for herself.

In her heart, Mandi believed that listening to her aunt's rants would make this woman happier. Or maybe it would somehow show loyalty to her dead grandma. Or maybe her submissiveness would be adequate payment for the checks. But Aunt Mary's happiness and her generosity were in her circle of responsibility, not Mandi's.

Have you ever had a relationship in which you felt like you were responsible for the other person's happiness? Write that person's name here. How did you try to take over God's job of caring for this person? In a couple of sentences, summarize the situation. What disaster occurred when you felt responsible for another person's joy?

_____

_____

_____

_____

Your Sins are Your Sins

The other way most of us confuse boundaries is that we feel like we're doing a loved one a favor by shielding them from the natural consequences of their actions. Aunt Mary didn't have many friends because she could be stubborn, belligerent, belittling, and grumpy. Instead of gently telling her aunt that she didn't like how she treated her, Mandi silently endured the treatment. And even though I suspect Aunt Mary knew exactly which of Mandi's buttons she was pushing with the passive-aggressive "fat" comments, she spared her aunt the real lesson by putting up with them.

If Mandi had stood up to Aunt Mary much sooner, it may have been the wake-up call the other woman needed to try harder in her other relationships.

Like a riverbank that directs the water flow in a different way, a boundary can set another person's actions in a different direction. This other person is still responsible for herself, but you give her a little nudge to show her what doesn't work with other people. ("When you show up late, I feel like you don't care about my schedule." "When you gossip like that, it makes me worried that you also gossip about me." "When you lose your temper at our son's football games, it embarrasses us and we don't want to go with you.")

Oftentimes, we want our people to avoid getting cut on life's hard edges, but shielding is not always the kindest way to help them. Indulging a person with poor boundaries isn't an honest relationship. You are an active part of letting them wash over a place where there should be a natural turn in their tide. When you don't stand up and say, "Your out-of-control spending means you will have to sell your car," but instead you keep loaning your son money, you're covering up an organic and important learning opportunity.

Plus, if you're doing life with a person with poor boundaries, you will often find yourself as part of their circus. Case in point, our kids are sensitive and have big feelings. Oftentimes (okay, almost every meal), one of them comes to the table with a bellyful of pain about something. One of our daughters is feeling hurt about some drama that went down at recess, and she will fling herself down to her pot roast with a scowl on her face. She will glare at her brother when he crunches his cauliflower too loudly. Then she will start with the, "Can you *please* chew with your mouth closed?"

When I'm tired and my boundaries are poor, I will totally get sucked into this kind of behavior. Yes, she is being ugly to other members of my family. But my desire to help her will cloud my judgment. Instead of telling her she can choose between being kind to us or eating her dinner in the dining room, I'll ask everyone to chew more quietly for her. I'll pour her a glass of her favorite juice. I'll take her side in her story of the playground politics. Her bad mood has become my responsibility, and I will feel really bad right alongside her, in hopes that a compliant, bad-feeling mama might be a bright spot in her day.

I ask you, what kind of insane logic is this?

We all know what happens next because this is probably the scene going on around many of our dinner tables. My daughter has learned that chiding others for their chewing gives her power. Pouting means more attention and more juice. Suddenly, we're all operating on a nine-year-old's understanding of social relationships. *Everyone else is wrong, and she is always the self-righteous victim.*

As the dinner unravels, everyone is now caught up in the circus of these emotions. She is becoming more and more bossy, and everyone is more and more tense. Instead of using this as a chance to help her understand that telling other people off and whining are two qualities that will ensure you get picked on tomorrow at recess, we are enabling her to act like this.

What kind of genuine family support is this?

Have you been an enabler to someone's bad behavior? Write about a relationship with a person who has abused money or drugs or power or you. Why didn't you stand up to this person? Write about the emotions that kept you from putting up a boundary for him or her.

Don't Get to the Breaking Point

A problem with poor boundaries—with Aunt Mary or my strong-willed daughter or the situation you might be involved with right now with your own brother or mother—is that they are built on half-truths. By not standing up to the person, you're telling him, "You can't deal with reality."

You're teaching him, "You can't handle the truth that your overeating really is damaging your health," or "Your smoking is causing all of your other medical problems," or "Your sarcasm hurts other people's feelings."

Essentially, you are saying to your brother or your mother, "I will handle that for you because I believe you're too weak to deal with the reality yourself." Really, you're telling your family members, "I don't have enough trust that God will take care of you. So I will try to do it all myself."

But because you are not God, you will not be able to handle their problems. And definitely not forever. At some point, you will throw their bad habits back at them and say, "I can't deal with this. You need to handle your own mess."

Inevitably the other person—the one who has sort-of worshiped you as her own personal savior—will be very unhappy about this. Because she will have seen you as the one who took care of her, the only one who understands, the only one who cares enough to enable her.

When you stop, this other person will (rightfully) be confused. Because she understood you to be someone you never could really be. You were acting as the caretaker of her circle of responsibility. And who wants to take responsibility for themselves again after they've been on sabbatical for so long?

Suddenly, your sister or mother or daughter is going to realize that she doesn't have any friends or money or job left. She's going to need someone to blame for this. You might be that target. Once she idolized you for being the only one who understood or loaned her money or didn't criticize her. But now that she's pushed to the point that you can't take it anymore, you push back. This is a terrible place for both of you to be.

For this reason, don't be afraid to be the natural boundary in someone else's life. Trust that God will provide what your family member needs on the deepest levels. You can love and pray for her, but if what she's asking you to take on is within her circle of responsibility, tell this person exactly that: "I can't loan you money anymore because this is what my husband and I are saving for retirement." "If you are talking ugly to other members of this family, you will eat alone in the dining room." "I would like to visit you on Saturday mornings, but I need to bring my kids with me." "Mom, I can host the family Christmas breakfast, but I've been fighting this cold, so I need to rest. I'll have to scale the party way back this year."

When you redefine your boundaries, you help to create a culture of grace in your family. When each person is responsible for his or her own choices, the family can all function as individuals. This naturally helps to remove the hurt feelings and resentments that come with poor boundaries.

Again, God is our ultimate caretaker, and He loves each and every one of His children perfectly. Setting up as a natural boundary helps others to know when they are violating your circle of responsibility. This is when boundaries can help foster better relationships within your family, your family tree, and your family of Christ.

Chances are that you've experienced some rough breaking points in your relationships. Maybe this happened with a first boyfriend or in an early, immature friendship. Or, maybe, you're struggling with a boundary right now. Write about a breaking point you've had with someone because of poor boundaries. What wisdom have you learned here?

_____

_____

_____

_____

_____

THE PICTURE OF GOD'S PERFECT CARE

When you find yourself struggling with boundaries in your family, trust the perfect ways that God cares for you and takes care of everyone else. You are like a very sick child, lying in bed with a stomachache full of sin, scared about ever standing up again. You're chilly with a fever and desperate for the doctor to give you something to heal you.

This is where your heavenly Father, the wisest doctor in the world, steps in to sit on your bed and hold your hand. He has the right prescription, the right salve, and is the perfect company. This is how it feels to be cared for by the very best Physician. You can trust this. He is the Healer.

You know about this care because you've experienced it your whole life. He has given you the right timing for important lessons. Your heavenly Father has given you the right skills and exact people you need to make major changes. Although you couldn't have guessed it years ago, He's blessed you with the exact right family at His perfect timing.

Not only that, God will never, ever leave your bedside. He doesn't get tired of sitting there and He doesn't need a break. He doesn't suddenly remember another patient and rush off to help him. He doesn't get exasperated with your sickness or tell you that He'll come back when you're in a better mood or you can pay the bill.

Here's the craziest news: He is doing this kind of radical care for every single person—for every single person in your family. Sometimes, He's caring for them by giving them new opportunities. And, sometimes, He's closing down opportunities. Sometimes, He is caring for them by encouraging them with sweet seasons of celebration and progress. And, sometimes, He's walking them through the very hardest seasons of their lives.

And although you would do absolutely anything to take that burden from your loved one, that's not your job. God is right there with this person you love, and He is walking through every step and giving her the perfect nutrients and experiences and realizations to equip her.

It's not your responsibility (or ability) to come in as her savior. If this person rejects the Holy Spirit and His perfect care, you can't change her heart. You can only love her, listen, and pray for her.

And trust the real Physician, your heavenly Father.

Write about a family member going through a really hard season. What does it feel like to stand by? Write out a prayer that asks God to take care of him or her and to help you support him or her in a healthy way.

_____

_____

_____

_____

DENISE AND CHAD: A MOTHER AND SON ON NEW TERMS

As our family has tried to learn more about a culture of grace, I'm trying to understand how I can have better boundaries with my family. It's going—okay.

Most days, I feel like I'm in elementary school when it comes to loving my family with good boundaries. In some seasons, I show co-dependent levels of communication. During these times, I feel completely responsible for the success and failure of the people I love.

But then, my parents or in-laws need me to do something I don't have the time or energy for, and I feel like a failure. I try to tell them no, but I do it awkwardly and fumbling. Then, because I feel guilty, I will often just take care of it, full of resentment. They're frustrated and so am I, and I'm back to Pre-K in my ability to show good boundaries. Circle of responsibility? Ha. My boundaries look like giant orbs of everyone's jobs. I'm learning, though. Kind of.

But my friend Denise has been through some of the hardest boundary lessons. She has earned a PhD in when to walk away, when to run, and when to stay. For Denise, the hardest boundary has been the one she's had to establish with her son, Chad.

First, Denise loves her family with the kind of passion that often makes me want to claim myself as her relative just so I can enjoy the unconditional love and support she shines at her sons and her daughters.

But Chad has been different. Even though Denise has offered him the very best that she has, he has rejected her. He argues, he's insulting, and he defies her rules.

Eventually, Denise had to establish some boundaries about how he talks to her and how he treats the rest of the family. These have been the worst kind of discussions—Chad yelling hateful words and Denise telling him he can't talk to her like that. She has prayed for Chad endlessly, seen counselors about their relationship, and learned her hardest lessons about how good boundaries can hurt.

Now, Denise doesn't see Chad often. And, yet, she is so peaceful about this. When I sat down with her and asked how she dealt with this, she said, "Chad has a very independent nature. He has always wanted to explore all of life's challenges. Though his ideas are usually far different than what I would choose for him, I've learned through hard knocks that I do not want our love relationship harmed."

The love relationship that Denise has with Chad is rooted in her dual citizenship. She tries to love her son in the same way that God loves us—unconditionally and with radical grace. She tells Chad that he will always be her son. Even if they don't speak, they belong to each other forever.

Denise explains, "Through eyes of grace, I can see that Chad's different ideas are a by-product of what I taught him. We always encouraged independence and unconditional love in our family."

For Denise, part of having good boundaries is letting Chad walk off with Jesus and trusting that He is taking care of him. "Sometimes, there is hurt in the lack of relationship we have at this time. God has put it on my heart each morning to see him walk off with Jesus' arm around him—my Jesus that loves him more than I can think or imagine. This allows a mother to have peace in the present."

Absolutely beautiful.

May this be the promise and the picture that each and every one of us has when it comes to teaching unconditional love and independence to our family members.

We have the promise that God cares for us, better than we even realize or want or completely understand. He cares for others in ways that are surprising and counterintuitive and completely radical and exactly perfect.

Samantha: An Olive Branch Story of Hope in Family Boundaries

My friend Samantha works for a pro-life nonprofit. She is passionate, intelligent, and a hard worker. Through her career, she's spread the pro-life message to schools and churches, at rallies, and at peaceful protests. In today's complicated political climate, at a time when so many are confused or timid about sanctity of life issues, Samantha is a brave messenger of God's love for His treasured creation, His children.

Recently, Samantha moved from the Midwest to live with her great-aunt in San Francisco. Most of Samantha's aging aunts and uncles live in the Bay area, and Samantha wanted to help care for them. Plus, she had always loved the terrain of the West Coast and had dreamed of calling it home.

Samantha moved to San Francisco during the fiery election season of 2016. The media portrayed this election as men versus women—more specifically, as pro-life versus pro-choice. Samantha was not only a pro-life woman, her career took her to the front lines of this very public battle. In addition, she was doing this hard work in one of the most unchurched and politically-charged communities in our country. To say she felt rejected and out of place would be an understatement.

Mostly, she felt rejected right inside her new house. Samantha's great-aunt and uncle were passionate about politics—and, they were on the other side of the voting booth. When it came to sanctity of life issues, what Samantha saw as a spiritual issue, they saw as a political issue. She loved her family deeply—and she also completely disagreed with them on most major issues.

Just about the time that Donald Trump was elected president, and all of America was fighting on Facebook and on Main Street, Samantha was second-guessing her decision to move in with her aunt. The political debates drained her. As tempers flared all over America, Samantha was fighting political battles in her own household.

Within the span of a week, her aunt marched in the Women's March while Samantha marched for life. Then, Samantha gathered colleagues and friends to attend the March for Life, and her aunt didn't speak a kind word to her for a week.

Samantha has learned so much over this past nine months about boundaries and family love. She has learned to separate her relationship with her family from her passion for pro-life causes. She has learned self-control and when to speak her mind. She's had to come to her heavenly Father for unconditional love and acceptance, rather than looking for that from her family.

Through this season, God has reminded Samantha that she isn't responsible for changing anyone in her family. She can pray for them, love them, share her opinions, and care for them. But it's only God who can change their hearts.

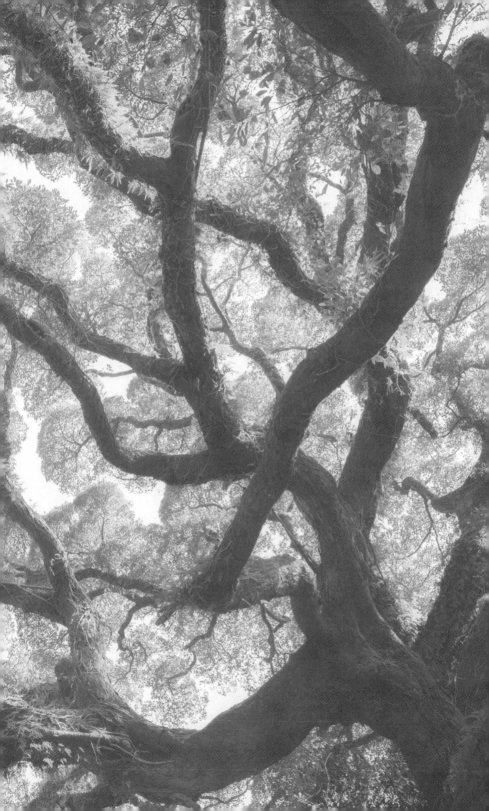

49 Olive Branches for Busy Families

Yes, our family is stuck in some bad habits. I only have to think back as far as breakfast and I cringe at how short-tempered we were with each other. Also, we're not putting the time into each other like I know we should. But, to be honest, I'm never sure where to start. Trying to make changes in how we treat each other seems overwhelming.

Ava, 43

For this reason I bow my knees before the Father, from whom every family in heaven and on earth is named, that according to the riches of His glory He may grant you to be strengthened with power through His Spirit in your inner being, so that Christ may dwell in your hearts through faith—that you, being rooted and grounded in love, may have strength to comprehend with all the saints what is the breadth and length and height and depth and to know the love of Christ that surpasses knowledge, that you may be filled with all the fullness of God. *Ephesians 3:14–19*

A Toolbox of Practical Ideas for Busy Families

When my in-laws were looking to buy a house several years ago, they found one with the perfect place for a stained glass window. My mother-in-law, Marcilee, loves doves, and so my father-in-law, Mark, commissioned an artist to create a dove stained glass window for a spot where morning sunlight floods into their house.

When the light shines through this window, the dove sparkles as a constant reminder of the Holy Spirit in their lives. It's one of my favorite parts of their home.

The window also serves as the beautiful reminder of what a culture of grace looks like in our families. Piece by piece, we build habits to show God's grace. His brilliant love shines through this mosaic of our colors to illuminate our little communities with His grace.

This last section is 49 little pieces of glass you can use to build a culture of grace in your home. These are habits you can start today or ones you can develop over generations.

Use these habits as live wires to jump-start a new culture of grace in your family. Trust that God's perfect love will shine through your efforts and illuminate the forgiveness in your lives.

ONE.

In a Forest of Family Trees, Yours Is Unique.
Celebrate Your Individuality!

Begin with the End in Mind.

> I have been crucified with Christ. It is no longer I who live, but Christ who lives in me. And the life I now live in the flesh I live by faith in the Son of God, who loved me and gave Himself for me.
>
> Galatians 2:20

When I suggested to my husband that our family write a mission statement, he gave me the same look he does when I suggest we adopt a third greyhound.

I pointed out that a family mission statement would help us clarify our values. "If we agreed about what's important, we could make quicker decisions for our family."

"A mission statement? They're so tedious," he argued.

I get it. Mission statements have gotten a bad rap. Writing one can feel like trying to recreate the United States Constitution in one long and awkward sentence. Boiling down your family's core values to one clear statement sounds like something a teacher would assign you; not the way you want to spend a Saturday morning with your family.

But whether or not you enjoy the process, writing a mission statement is hugely helpful in defining your family's identity. It bonds you together in a common goal. It enriches your culture. Life can feel like an adventure when your family is united in the same mission. And, yes, it gives you a framework for making more efficient decisions.

Write a mission statement that's short and clearly describes who you are. Here are effective mission statements: *The Schmidt Family Solves Problems and Comes Together to Pray. The Potter Family Shares with Those in Need. The Nolte Family Trusts God by Studying His Word. The Johnson Family Learns from Failure. The Hergenrader Family Wants to Live a Better Story That Is Filled with Grace.*

A good mission statement can include more branches of your family tree than the ones living in your house. You can print your mission statement on a little sign and hang it in your house. Or you can remind one another about it when your family is in conflict. Or when you don't know what to do next. Family mission statements can feel like a life preserver when your larger family is dealing with tidal waves of struggles.

One family I know printed their mission statement on T-shirts to wear at their family reunion: *The Jackson Family Shares the Seeds of Faith!*

We can all get behind a mission like that, can't we?

Your Vocation is Serving These People—Even During Holidays.

> But the fruit of the Spirit is love, joy, peace, patience, kindness, goodness, faithfulness, gentleness, self-control; against such things there is no law.
>
> Galatians 5:22–23

Let's talk about the four times a year that might be the most difficult for your family tree: Christmas, Thanksgiving, Easter, and Fourth of July.

Holidays gather together your family's introverts and extroverts, the Democrats and Republicans, the vegetarians and the hunters, the pastors and those who haven't been to church in months. When all these different people come together, it can feel a bit like a circus of personalities and opinions.

But God has put these people in your life as your family, as your neighbors—meaning the ones whom you are close to right now. This is not an accident or a coincidence. He calls you to love and serve this crazy hodgepodge of people.

Celebrate your role of service to these specific people at this specific moment. See what God wants you to learn from these men and women. Remember that He has placed them in your life for specific reasons and that you're in their lives for these reasons too.

Your family is a party sent to you by our loving, sovereign God. You get to be a unique and valuable part of this crazy, lovable group of your people. You get to be the one who shows the world what God's love feels like. You get to show the fruits of the Spirit through a tight hug, eye contact, hands clasped in prayer, the carbonated joy of laughter, lightening the load of someone who needs help.

These people might be a mess, but they're your mess. And you're theirs.

Hallelujah. Pass the green bean salad.

Bring a Love Generator to Those Who Need It.

> But to all who did receive Him, who believed in His name, He gave the right to become children of God.
>
> John 1:12

The next time your family is together, try to be the love generator to everyone—even to those in your family who might seem unlovable.

Ask God to remind you of your identity through Him. Remember . . . "I am God's child. This is why I'm valuable." Then, shine this love on everyone else, even the unlovable members of your family. They are God's children and need to feel His love too. Okay, especially your unlovable relatives need God's love. Hand out compliments and hugs and smiles like you're a politician and you have nothing to lose.

Because you really don't have anything to lose. You also don't have to wonder if these people deserve your kindness. You don't have to judge or worry about who is doing this for you or not doing that.

Instead, just do tons of love. Ask the Holy Spirit to flow through you like your soul is made of cheesecloth. Trust that this love you get to share comes from your infinite, creative, generous Father. Trust that He'll keep providing it.

Write down how this family event goes. What changed when you shared His love with your family who needs it? What was different with them? What about with you?

Keep Trying. Keep Forgiving. Keep Trusting. This Might Take a Long Time.

> Weeping may tarry for the night, but joy comes with the morning.
>
> Psalm 30:5

The most unique part of building a culture of grace in your family is how long it might take before anything changes in your house. Often it feels like God is taking the long way when it comes to leading your family to a place of love and forgiveness. In other words, resolving conflict and teaching deep forgiveness might take decades instead of an afternoon.

If you're going through desert days right now, remember this: the disciples believed that the Romans had won. After the resurrection, they were locked in the Upper Room and scared. They were second-guessing everything they had witnessed about Jesus. They were *mourning*.

And then? Then, Jesus showed up and absolutely blew everyone's minds by standing right there in front of them, showing the deep holes in His hands.

This moment changed everything for the rest of history. Those same dejected disciples got to jump up and touch the holes in their Savior's hands. Jesus' best friends got to smack their foreheads and say, "Ahh. This was the point. We couldn't really believe it. But, look! It's true. Easter is true. And that changes ETERNITY."

Pray for moments like this in your family. Pray for Easter-morning relationships in your little tribe, even if it feels as black as Friday night right now. See the water and manna God is sending to sustain you right now. Ask for faith to get through this hurting season.

Remember, joy comes in the morning.

Eat Some Sauerkraut with Your Sister.

> Not neglecting to meet together, as is the habit of some, but encouraging one another, and all the more as you see the Day drawing near.
> Hebrews 10:25

Most of the men and women I talked to report spending very little time with their adult siblings. This is a modern phenomenon. Now that families live farther apart, most grown siblings say they find it very hard to connect with one another. Considering that your brothers and sisters were once the closest people to you, the most important ones in your life, this distance is a disappointment for your family tree.

God created you to connect, and if you're not connecting with your siblings, you might be in some phase of disconnecting. This also means you're modeling these estrangements to the next generation.

As you're trying to raise the next generation in a culture of grace and unity, find ways to connect with your adult siblings. Schedule times with your brothers and sisters to do something everyone likes to do. To do this, you can ask yourself, and your siblings, "Who have we become and what do we still have in common?"

Maybe you all grew up to love the sauerkraut your German grandma made, and no one else you know will go near the stuff. Meet up with your sisters at the German polka restaurant to feast on Hefeweizen and bratwurst.

This is connection. This is modeling a culture of grace to the next generation. This is living in the joyful connection of something you all love.

Find Your Family Fun.

> A time to weep, and a time to laugh; a time to mourn, and a time to dance.
>
> Ecclesiastes 3:4

Mini-golf at midnight. Cinema night to binge watch all the great baseball movies. A Color Run 5K in white T-shirts. Taking the dogs to run through the pond at the pet park. A dance-off in the living room. Family book club. Shopping together.

Doing something that makes multiple generations snort with laughter is absolutely one of the gifts God has given us as part of His gift of family. Figure out what your family fun is and go do it.

Finding your fun is a wonderful way to celebrate together how your family is different than any other. Your family fun is a combination of your mixed passions and shared experiences. It's the activities that make you laugh. It's the things you do so everyone can relax. It's your own brand of recreation that is peaceful and exhilarating and ensures that everyone keeps showing up.

If you all love to play games together, then meet up on Friday nights around the Monopoly board like it's your job. If it's movies that your family loves, get a Netflix subscription and a long list of everyone's favorites. Promise to show up every Sunday night because this is part of your family identity.

You're not only showing your people that they are important, but you're also celebrating what makes you a family: shared experiences, preferred values, and your commitment to making future memories together.

Family > Solo.

> What then, brothers? When you come together, each one has a

> hymn, a lesson, a revelation, a tongue, or an interpretation. Let all things be done for building up.
>
> 1 Corinthians 14:26

You already know the power of groupthink because you've been part of a family—the very first kind of a brainstorming group—your whole life. You have had the wise counsel of loving input from the brigade of aunts and uncles and cousins and grandparents in your life. These people are God's free gift to you—your own focus group for fixing problems in your life.

But the corporate world is just catching up on how important it is to consult a group before making a decision. Recently, there's been much attention and excitement about the power of lots of people working together to solve a problem. When a group gets together, it's the shading and blending of sharp perspectives. We're just now starting to realize how important cooperative learning is: "You're wrong about some of that, and I'm wrong about a little of this. But together, we're closer to being right."

In other words, when you're making a decision about when Mom needs to move into assisted living or Dad needs cataract surgery, it's good to talk to everyone. The sister who never speaks up might be the one with the best insight.

Gather together and ask opinions. You'll be surprised by the wisdom and perspectives from your unique clan.

Two.

Dinner Together and Dancing in the Kitchen are Water and Sunlight for Your Family Tree. Gather Your Family Together!

> For where two or three are gathered in My name, there am I among them.
>
> Matthew 18:20

Every Fourth of July, my mother-in-law gathers us to pose for hundreds of family pictures. The whole deal—hours in the blinding sun, wearing itchy clothes, grinning like we're in a toothpaste commercial—seems like something her family, especially her sons, would boycott.

She doesn't apologize or give us a choice, though. And guess what? All twelve of us show up at the assigned park with picture-perfect smiles. Even the nine-year-old boy cousins pose for the morning of photos. And they do it happily.

Why? Because family pictures are Grandma's passion and we know that. Every year, my mother-in-law prints all the pictures and hangs them around her house because they give her so much pleasure. Her grandkids tease her for this ("Grandma has seventy-five family pictures of me in her house!"). Grandma has unabashedly established this as a family tradition.

My aunt and uncle have made homemade pizza every Friday night for the past fifty years. Their six kids and several grandkids—and now even their great-grandkids—gather for it every week. For decades, they have rolled the crust out onto bent cookie sheets, spread the homemade sauce on lumpy dough, then covered a few with green chilies, others with hamburger, and still others with a deck of pepperoni slices.

Family traditions are a surprisingly easy way to solidify your culture and show you care about this group of people. It's insurance you'll see one another often. It's a chance to gather and check on everyone. It's a scheduled intergenerational meet and greet. It's a chance to be the hands and feet of Jesus to the neighbors nearest to your heart.

What tradition can you start in your family? What do you love that you can share with the people you love? Schedule an activity and try it for a year or a decade and see what new roots you can plant in your family tree.

Food = Family Glue.

> There is nothing better for a person than that he should eat and drink and find enjoyment in his toil. This also, I saw, is from the hand of God.
>
> Ecclesiastes 2:24

Gathering together around your family table is some of the very best sunshine and water you can give your family tree.

Circling around the table for good food is nourishment for both your bodies and for your souls. When the family comes together, clanking their forks and reaching for seconds, and telling the stories of their lives, they are caring for one another in both the most basic and the most sophisticated ways.

Find some special foods for these generations of your family tree. Maybe it's Grandma's potatoes, the ones with the hash browns and cream of mushroom soup. Or a treasured recipe that's been handed down for generations. Or, as one of my dearest friends says, "All our family's favorite foods come from restaurants. When we gather, it's at Olive Garden. Or for the best carnitas tamales in Houston. It's the food that bonds us together, not who made it."

Awesome. Pasta and chimichangas will still be around in the next decade. When the next generation gathers, they can order green enchiladas in the name of sweet Grandma Evelyn, who loved them. Then, the cousins can pass around the chips and salsa and toast another great year together.

Show up.

> And day by day, attending the temple together and breaking bread in their homes, they received their food with glad and generous hearts.
>
> Acts 2:46

Showing up is one of those little acts that ends up being a big one. Especially in families. As you've probably already discovered, so much of maintaining relationships is just being there.

Coming to a family gathering covers a multitude of sins. Just saying yes to the invitation is the gravy you pour over the lumpy mashed potatoes. Accepting the invitation is the frosting you smear on the lopsided cake. Showing up to the birthday party your black sheep cousin is having for her daughter is one step toward a culture of grace in your family.

Sure, you might have that weird argument going on with your brother, but go to his second wedding anyway. Smile for the pictures. Hug his new wife. Bring a gift. Pray for their marriage. Tell your niece that Jesus loves her. Smile and mean it. God will take care of the details. Your job is to show up.

God sent His flesh-and-blood Son to earth to live as an actual man, to have real relationships with other flesh-and-blood people. On the epic, divine level, Jesus *showed up* and lived shoulder to shoulder with other humans. (Of course, He died for them too. And in that way, He showed up in a way like no one else could.)

But He also showed up at family gatherings and time with His friends and for weddings and funerals.

You should too.

Hold Family Meetings.

> Behold, how good and pleasant it is when brothers dwell in unity!
>
> Psalm 133:1

In our house, we have started meeting on Sunday nights, so we could give our kids more of a voice about how our family works together. Instead of a "waterfall" approach, the one where the parents dictate bedtime, how we'll spend our weekends, and what kind of snacks I should buy, we ask the kids what's going well and what we need to improve. This is like an avalanche of grace because everyone feels loved and valued.

I'm happy to report these family meetings are absolutely working. Our four kids are surprisingly insightful about how we can improve our schedule, our meals, and our bad habits.

Just this week, they've come up with a solution for us to get out the door earlier in the mornings ("Can you wake us up ten minutes earlier?"), how to make bedtime go smoother ("I think it would help if you could sit in my room, so I remember not to turn my light on and read"), and what we can do better ("Mommy, can you get in the carpool line earlier, so we have more time after school to finish our homework?").

Gather your family once a week to talk about issues, problems, or good things happening in your family. Refer to your mission statement and discuss how you're living it out.

Track the progress of projects. Ask the hard question, "How are we doing?", about everything your family does together: managing money, meeting together for meals, chores, getting out of the house on time, church, serving the community, doing your different vocations, and having fun together.

As you talk about these, give each family member an equal chance to share their opinions. You're a team here, working together to create the culture you want as you do life together.

Deep Nurturing to the Roots.

> A new commandment I give to you, that you love one another:
> just as I have loved you, you also are to love one another. By this all
> people will know that you are My disciples, if you have love for one
> another."
>
> John 13:34–35

Although huge Easter egg hunts and family gatherings at Christmas Eve services are a fantastic way for your family to gather as a large group, quiet time together, one-on-one, is where the deepest bonding happens.

Consider this. When you're falling in love with someone, you want to spend all kinds of time with him away from the rest of the world. You want to understand who he is and how he thinks. You want to experience fun adventures together, just so you can see the way it makes his face light up.

Without anyone telling you, "This is the path to a better relationship," you know that the deepest bonding comes when it's just the two of you, looking each other in the eyes, and learning about each other, one-on-one.

This is the same for every relationship, especially family ones. Take your son to a Major League Baseball game, just the two of you. Write him notes to tell him what you enjoy about him. Talk through issues you're having. Separate from the rest of the group and experience something remarkable with just the two of you.

Share your faith with your daughter. Honestly share your struggles and also your fears. Describe the ways you see God working in your family.

Alone. Together. One-on-one.

(Maybe) the Most Important Part of the Tree.

> Honor your father and your mother, as the LORD your God com-
> manded you, that your days may be long, and that it may go well
> with you in the land that the LORD your God is giving you.
>
> Deuteronomy 5:16

If you're in the same stage I'm in right now (the trunk of our deep-rooted family tree, nurturing the newest buds), you know that the grandparent roots in your family can feel like a specific blessing created especially for your little tribe.

The people I interviewed had so much praise for the wonderful blessing of grandparents, specifically how they help nurture grace in their families. They reported that grandparents . . .

- were the wisest teachers to model selflessness, grace, forgiveness, and unconditional love;

- noticed a health or emotional issue with their grandkids before they (the parents) had noticed it;

- shared more similarities with their grandkids than with their kids, proving the truth that many passions, gifts, and interests "skip a generation;"

- served as important messengers of the Gospel to their grandkids;

- provided significant financial help to their kids and grandkids;

- discovered they enjoyed being grandparents more than they enjoyed being parents.

Wow. Can we all agree that the concept of grandparents is really genius planning on God's part? Here are these people, who love your kids as much as you do, and they're in the stage of life when they have extra leisure time and money and so much love for the same people you love.

Grandparents are like live wires of love and grace and the Gospel, flowing straight from the roots of your family tree, through the trunk, and to the newest buds.

If you're the trunk of the family tree—the connector between generations—nurture this special relationship that will bless both generations.

Fail, Faith, & Forgive.

> Let all bitterness and wrath and anger and clamor and slander be put away from you, along with all malice. Be kind to one another, tenderhearted, forgiving one another, as God in Christ forgave you.
> Ephesians 4:31–32

From all the families I've talked to for this book, I've learned the importance of messing up together. Failure, for as much as we fear it, really does end up teaching us the very best lessons.

When your kids see you fail, or when you see your siblings (their aunts and uncles) fail and then try again, it's a huge relief for the whole, blessed family tree. It's permission to not be perfect. It's instruction about how to ask for forgiveness and how to give it.

It's a powerful example to see how your parents react when they fail. In fact, of everything you can teach your kids about grace, showing them how to learn from failure could be the one that teaches them the very best.

So rewrite your family's narrative from "We've always been good at . . . " to "With God's help, we try hard to . . . ." This inserts grace right in the middle of the family tree. Instead of heaping unreasonable expectations on your kids, this teaches them that they only have to try.

The lessons of failing teach faith that God will help you to do better next time. And this is a chance to taste the sweet taste of forgiveness.

THREE.

How is the Weather over There?
Communicate with Your Family!
What to Do with Family Secrets?

> Fear not, for you will not be ashamed; be not confounded, for you will not be disgraced.
>
> Isaiah 54:4

Every family has stories covered in secrecy. Interviewing men and women for this book was sometimes a challenge because some of the stories they wanted to share were in the classified file of their family history. I felt their tension as I talked to them. There was so much they wanted to explain—but also so much that they couldn't say.

As they talked, I could see them biting back the stories they were afraid to tell. Sometimes, they did tell them. *These are horrible words Mom yelled at me during that fight. . . . I found out that my grandma had actually gone to stay in the mental hospital. . . . The real reason that my aunt almost left my uncle is because he was having an affair. . . . Great-Aunt Maggie's death was a suicide.*

Some of the people I interviewed who shared these secrets with their families discovered the relief that comes from saying them out loud. These men and women had done the hard work: telling the secrets and understanding the lessons that from their rich and storied history. They had forgiven or they had asked for forgiveness. Here's what they told me about the process: telling the family secrets—speaking about the unspeakable—can be really helpful in your relationships.

Secrets can hold a power over your family. *Not* talking about the unspeakable events of the past has both the power to unify (those bonded in keeping these secrets) and the power to divide (those left out of the secret). But for overall family communication, one of the most important parts of a highly functioning family is to allow each member their own freedom to talk about whatever they want. The best communication means discussing what feels undiscussable.

Runs in the Family.

> A friend loves at all times, and a brother is born for adversity.
>
> Proverbs 17:17

Think about this: your extended family is your single most valuable resource about your own health. Their experiences and health history can serve as a living, breathing analysis of your own DNA.

The importance of talking about genetic health concerns is another case for open communication. Through these discussions, you're able to understand the health crises that plague your family gene pool. You can help the next generation understand how to deal with your specific body type or mental health vulnerabilities. You can talk about how they can use their unique physical strengths.

Write down everything you know about the physical and mental circumstances of your family tree. Write about which of the roots in your family tree struggled with gout or arthritis or alcoholism or bipolar disorder. Type it up and email it to your family.

Genetics are a blessing from God, one that might make you exclaim, "Oh, wow. I am connected to my people by much more than just a name and the Christmas mornings we've spent together for the past twenty years. I have her same nose and perfect pitch, her tendency to get sunburned and markers for breast cancer. These really are my people in every way."

Tell the Family Tales of Success. And Failure.

> The LORD our God be with us, as He was with our fathers. May He not leave us or forsake us.
>
> 1 Kings 8:57

One of the very best gifts you can give the next generation is insight into who they are in their sprawling, ancient, storied family tree.

Tell the next generation all the stories: the good and the bad and the ugly. These stories will teach them that they are part of something bigger, a larger group, a branch in the history of this specific clan.

Stories teach the youngest buds that they will one day be the roots for a future generation. They show your kids and grandkids that they are the newest part of the sacred, rich, important cycle of your family.

Tell the stories that teach them, "This is who we are—artists, rebels, entrepreneurs, teachers, southerners, Christians, farmers, hard workers, dreamers, lawyers, musicians, truth-tellers, volunteers, immigrants, baseball players."

Set up intentional times when generations of your family are together. When you're with different branches of your family tree, bring up parts of your parents' past. Invite everyone to tell their stories.

This is how the next generation learns this truth: "Wow! Part of my personality belongs to people I will never know." This is how the next generation starts to cherish themselves as the connector between the past and the future.

This is where you teach the newest family members that God has grown your sprawling family tree over decades and centuries and has intentionally given you to one another.

Take the First Step to Communicate with Family.

> If anyone says, "I love God," and hates his brother, he is a liar; for he who does not love his brother whom he has seen cannot love God

whom he has not seen.

1 John 4:20

On every level—physical, emotional, spiritual, and historical—we are deeply connected to the family that God gave us. We know the love in our family to be true, to be sacred, to be biblical, to be from God.

Unfortunately, because we live in such a messy, messed-up, sinful world, so much of our family life is filled with miscommunications. We really don't want this to be the case, but this is what relationships often look like. We just don't understand one another very well.

To clear up miscommunications, you might have to be the one to take the first step. I know how hard it is to pick up the three-hundred-pound phone, but, many times, this first step is also the last step. Talking to the person who hurt your feelings often works to resolve your conflict before it really starts.

This is a culture of grace. This is you taking the first step in the name of better family relationships. This is living connected to the generations of those in your family who are gone and those who are yet to come.

The Family that Prays Together.

Again I say to you, if two of you agree on earth about anything they ask, it will be done for them by My Father in heaven.

Matthew 18:19

When you sit down together as a family, take time to thank God for your meal. Jesus did this when He fed the 5,000 and at the Last Supper. If Jesus shows us it's important to thank God before a meal—if He takes the time to do it before these significant events—then this is also a good idea to do before you eat your soup at Panera.

This is another one of those ways that God gives us habits that help us take care of ourselves physically, emotionally, and spiritually. Praying together as a family is a fantastic way to connect with those who are most important in your life. Praying together before a meal establishes your traditions, unifies you in your experience, and humbles you as you recognize God as your ultimate Provider.

Plus, praying together can be fun. There are as many different family prayers as there are families. Some sing to the tune of the Scooby-Doo theme song, others recite the same words their great-grandparents did. In other families, the parent speaks a blessing over the kids. In still other families, the kids are the ones who say the prayer. And that can be very inspirational. (And very short.)

Highs and Lows.

> Your offspring shall be like the dust of the earth, and you shall spread abroad to the west and to the east and to the north and to the south, and in you and your offspring shall all the families of the earth be blessed.
>
> Genesis 28:14

Your family scatters for the day and then gathers again at the end of it. As you've probably found, the coming back together part can be the most challenging. While your family was apart, each of them has been fighting their own battles, getting beat up by the world, and building upon their own identities and individualities.

Here is a tried and true practice that helps families slide back into We after a day of Me. Try the game of High/Low. Ask one another, "What was the best part of your day? What do you wish would have gone better?"

More than just doing this with the people gathered around the dinner table, you can do this with all the branches of your family tree. When you see your parents for the monthly pizza night, start by going around the room and asking everyone, "What was your highlight of April? What was the lowest part of Lent for you?"

In the same way this works in the small circle of your immediate family, it's effective within the larger group too. Your family can plug back into the rest of the group by looking one another in the eyes and saying, "How are you really doing?"

This opens up so many levels of communication between all the limbs in your family tree. The next question you ask could be, "How can I pray for you?"

Coming together with the same people on a regular basis and admitting challenges and successes is family glue. Learning to tell how you messed up, learning to accept responsibility instead of teaching to blame . . . these are aspects of your culture of grace.

Dinner Time Totally Matters. Except Not the Food. Or the Time.

> Your wife will be like a fruitful vine within your house; your children will be like olive shoots around your table.
>
> Psalm 128:3

You've probably heard the research about how important it is for your family to eat dinner together. All the experts agree that, without a doubt, meeting for dinner together as a family is one of the most vital ways you can connect and communicate.

In your quest to create a culture of grace in your family, dinner is the time-out your people need to pray together, to encourage one another, to hear one another, to strengthen your identity as a group. This is the time for bonding; these are your best opportunities for grace.

The good news here is that your family still reaps the benefits of family meals even if you skip some of the rules. For example, families have found that the time of the meal doesn't matter at all. Sunday lunch counts, and so does strawberry shortcake at nine o'clock on a Friday night.

What *does* matter is gathering around the table and sharing stories and catching up on one another's lives. You can do this. Frozen pizza and store-bought cookies count. Gather to eat brownies straight from the pan or for Pop-Tarts and microwave bacon. Talk. Share. Connect, Connect, Connect.

Reportedly, the Kennedy kids (that would be Jack, Robert, and Ted) had to bow to their mother and recite poetry at their father's command. They came to the table prepared for debate on world politics. If these future politicians couldn't contribute to the conversation, their dad, Joe, scolded them.

You don't have to do any of that. Just ask everyone if they know any jokes and then to share the story of one time they laughed that day.

Four.

Prune and Prevent Further Infection.
Practice Good Conflict Resolution for Family Feuds!

In a Culture of Grace—Fight Fair.

> Do all things without grumbling or disputing, that you may be blameless and innocent, children of God without blemish in the midst of a crooked and twisted generation, among whom you shine as lights in the world.
>
> Philippians 2:14–15

Part of growing a family tree of olive branches is recognizing that you'll often have to prune the infections that threaten to take down the whole tree. In other words, it's so important to talk out the arguments in your family. And it's important to fight fair.

Good conflict resolution means starting where both of you agree. First, look for common ground and ways you can agree.

Most of the good in an argument comes during the first five minutes. Everything that needs to be said is often said then. After that, both people start to rewind further and further back into unrelated history, looking for ammunition.

This is when your discussions can get ugly. This is where you can go digging around in the soil of past fights—toxic soil that contains no nutrients for your current discussion.

Instead of this, tell your people exactly what you feel right now about this situation. Then, look for a mutual resolution. Don't be afraid to negotiate here or admit you're wrong. Remember, conflict resolution is a means to a better relationship, not an exercise in proving you're right.

And watch your language. Stay away from sarcasm. (It never helps.)

Also, here are words that typically mean you're not looking for a solution, but trying to defend yourself: "you always," "every time you," or "you never," or "you better stop," and "I won't."

When you hear yourself using phrases like this, take a short breather. Go to the bathroom and pray. Or offer to pray with the other person. (For the record, offering to pray with the other person is like grad-school level of relationships. Most of us stay in kindergarten when it comes to olive branches. We are doing the best we can just to stay connected and not run away from the ugly feelings that come with fighting with family.)

Fight fairly and you might find that much less of your time is spent in conflict. You might find that you resolve arguments more quickly and move on to olive branches more easily.

Forgive Quickly.

> Be angry and do not sin; do not let the sun go down on your anger.
>
> Ephesians 4:26

You might not even realize it, but when you are in a fight with a family member, a low-grade agitation scratches around in your soul.

Here's how it feels when you're feuding with someone you love: It's like grains of sands between your sheets. As you're weeding the garden, or texting a friend, or running a bath for your kids, that sand keeps scratching.

One part of *your self* (your spirit) is completely wrapped up in this conflict with your family member. This is infection. This is festering. This is not what God intended.

This is why God makes repentance and forgiveness so clear to us in the Bible. He tells us that when He forgives us, it's like removing our sin so far from us, it's the east from the west (see Psalm 103:12), that we're cleaned so thoroughly, it's like we are as white as snow (see Isaiah 1:18).

God is so completely forgiving because He knows we need to receive and understand mercy in absolute terms. This is the gift of a gracious God, of living as children of the Father who sent Jesus as an absolute, 100-percent payment for our sins. End the fight for this feeling of relief. No more scratching in your soul. When you've forgiven, and you've been forgiven, it's over.

The Best Truth about Family and Creating a Culture of Grace.

> Love is patient and kind; love does not envy or boast; it is not arrogant.
>
> 1 Corinthians 13:4.

When you have a conflict with your son or daughter or mother or cousin or brother, you will feel 110-percent certain that you are absolutely right. And your brother will feel 110-percent certain that he is absolutely right.

Everyone else in the family will see that the truth is someplace in the middle.

Actually, there are as many sides to the conflict you're having with your brother as there are people in your family. Because even when you feel so self-righteous about your opinion, even when you're convinced that Jesus Himself would agree with you, your other family members still love your brother too. They know you both well enough to see your shadings of the truth.

Like the judicial branch of the government, there are all kinds of definitions of truth and shades of justice in a family. Even though many people will listen to your side and nod and sympathize with you, others will be listening to your brother, nodding and helping him too.

This is another place where God's design is perfect. Because when everyone sees all the sides of the story, it helps you to realize that there are no villains and heroes here. Just many different stories and feelings and definitions of grace and forgiveness and understanding.

Ask God to help you see these multiple viewpoints as a blessing from Him. Try to talk to the other person one-on-one. Go to that meeting with the specific purpose of hearing his side. Ask the Holy Spirit to protect your heart and share with you the truth of what this other person is saying to you. Ask God for your goal to be to learn something new. Ask the Holy Spirit to move your heart toward forgiveness.

And thank God for the system of family, that sees and knows you and your blind spots—and loves you anyway.

Brain Stem Vs. Frontal Lobe (Or, the Lesson of the Monkeys).

> And I will give you a new heart, and a new spirit I will put within you. And I will remove the heart of stone from your flesh and give you a heart of flesh.
>
> Ezekiel 36:26

One of my friends, who works in mental health, makes monkey noises to herself whenever she finds her thoughts are coming from her brain stem (reactive reasoning) instead of from her frontal lobe (which is where rational thoughts begin).

My friend talks a lot about how we as humans are God's only creation that can understand the difference between these two. This means, of course, that we have the opportunity to use this ability for higher-level reasoning—especially when it comes to relationships. Double especially in our relationships with our families.

The first step for higher reasoning in your relationships is to realize what you can and cannot control. You cannot control another person's behavior. You cannot make your aunt stop drinking. You cannot make your toddler son go potty. You cannot make your grandma accept your sister again. You cannot force your cousin to quit telling everyone the details of her recent experience with natural childbirth.

When another family member's behavior is making you crazy is when you've stopped nurturing a family tree of olive branches. This is when you're screeching like a monkey in one of the branches. You're no longer thinking rationally; you're reacting.

But here's what you can do—you can pray and ask God to change your spirit about the situation. You can remember that He is their heavenly Father too, and He loves each and every one of your family members just as much as He loves you. He is taking perfect care of them, even if you don't see it. And His care is constant.

Also, you can ask God to help your aunt to stop drinking—and you can tell her you're praying for her and that you would be happy to watch her kids if she wants to go to an AA meeting.

You can pray for patience with potty training and to see this special time with your son as a blessing of your vocation. (You can also offer him a cookie for every successful trip to the potty.)

You can tell your grandma you love her and that you wish your family could spend more time together. You can pray for the Holy Spirit to change her heart.

You can pray for understanding (and a tough stomach) when your cousin starts the part of the story that goes, "and then I started to push."

Don't Be Afraid of Conflict.

> The LORD is near to the brokenhearted and saves the crushed in spirit.
>
> Psalm 34:18

Show me a family of three generations romping around Disney World, with everyone in their roles and functioning in the exact ways they always have, and I'll show you a family where pride and control are winning.

Now, show me a family two months after the matriarch has died, and no one knows if they should be making her old recipes or crying or getting Dad out of the house. Everyone is arguing about what Mom would have wanted and fighting over her antique china and the last of her strawberry pies in her freezer. All the kids are yelling and hurt and trying to forgive and praying for help and feeling confused. The grandkids are staying out of the way and hoping everyone would just hurry up and get back to normal.

There is pain and hurt and confusion in that family. And God's fingerprints are everywhere.

In other words, if you're in a tough season with your family (we are all in some kind of tough season with some family member), have faith! God might be working a slow, quiet miracle of love and grace. You can be sure that He will give you an opportunity for forgiveness. Through forgiving, you have the chance to learn the very best lessons in mercy, the ones that you'll fall back on for the rest of your life.

Most of all, Jesus is close to you right now. He is close to you all the time, but you probably recognize His presence differently when you're fighting the hardest battles.

This is part of the miracle of God becoming flesh to come to earth. Jesus sympathizes with our weaknesses (see Hebrews 4:15). He understands the sting of rejection, the sorrow of losing someone you love, the confusion of family in the wake of a conflict.

The realization that Jesus understands your pain and loves you through it might be the comfort you need to survive this darkest hour with your own family.

And it might open your eyes to the work God is already doing.

Imagine Your Fiftieth Anniversary.

> Commit your work to the Lord, and your plans will be established.
>
> Proverbs 16:3

To intentionally create a culture of grace in your family, try imagining your fiftieth anniversary. Let's say you have a party, and your whole family tree gathers around you to celebrate your marriage, and to also celebrate their deep, meaningful relationships. These are your people. This is your legacy and also the future of those you love more than anything else. As you sit around the table, what do you want the gathering to look like?

If you want people to truly know you, try to live a more vulnerable life. Be honest about how you're feeling, and don't be afraid to tell them how meaningful they are to you. Get to know them too. Do intentional activities, show up, and fall in love with who your kids and grandkids have become.

Care about resolving conflict and celebrating your family members. This is your family, one of the most significant blessings in your past, present, and future.

Most of all, forgive and be forgiven. Let grace flow between and through your branches. Ask the Lord to equip you for the hardest types of forgiveness. Don't underestimate God's ability to restore relationships here. The ones who are separated from your family tree right now might be the ones sitting right next to you next year.

Imagine this party to celebrate your marriage to your spouse, and also the olive branches God has grown all over your family tree.

Focus on the Present.

> Therefore do not be anxious about tomorrow, for tomorrow will be anxious for itself. Sufficient for the day is its own trouble.
>
> Matthew 6:34

Yes, you've known this person forever. Yes, this is the same family member who will likely be part of your life for the rest of all of your days. Yes, you could list every one of his faults—all the way back to that time he lied in the third grade. As tempting as it is to focus on the enormity of all this past and all that future, don't. This is actually not a fantastic time to mention that you really have never trusted him. Actually, this isn't a helpful time to even *think* that.

Because you can't bring any of the decades of the past or the decades of the future into today's argument. The conflict you're trying to resolve today is enough for today. Not what happened last year or what might happen in the next month. This is what Jesus taught in Matthew 6:34. Your mind and spirit can't handle the spanning years. Let today's conflict be enough.

When you work out family fights, boil the conflict down to the most basic two sides happening right here and right now and limit your discussion to only that.

Nurturing a culture of grace means totally letting the past go. It means completely leaving the future to God. Yes, this is so hard.

Yes, it is so necessary to the health of your family tree.

FIVE.

Plant the Shade Trees for the Next Generation.
Teach Your Kids Grace and Gratitude!
Modeling an Attitude of Gratitude.

> But thanks be to God, who gives us the victory through our LORD
> Jesus Christ.   1 Corinthians 15:57

If you've been to Chick-fil-A, you know that the employees will always respond to every "thank you" and every request with, "my pleasure."

It's their pleasure to give me three extra packages of mixed nuts for my salad. It's their pleasure to open the door for me when my arms are full of kids' hands and cups of lemonade. It's their pleasure to take my son's sticky kid's meal toy and exchange it for an ice cream cone.

I would guess it's actually not their pleasure at all to do any of this. Their pleasure would be if this was the end of the shift and it was time to go home and smell something besides chicken. It would also be their pleasure to sit down at one of the booths and eat an ice cream sundae instead of making them all day.

Yet, the Chick-fil-A employees show the attitude of gratitude about everything. They have been trained to be grateful. It's part of the culture at Chick-fil-A and part of their job. They are grateful to help, grateful you've chosen chicken nuggets for lunch, grateful they have this job to serve you. Gratitude is the culture—and a choice—at Chick-fil-A.

Being grateful can also make a big difference in the Body of Christ too. This is a change in our hearts, which is actually the very hardest kind of change because it changes how you understand God and His gifts to you. Especially when His gifts aren't exactly what you asked for.

But you can be certain that God gives you what's best for you. He always has and He always will. Model gratitude for whatever God gives you. Show your family how to appreciate the blessings with a "my pleasure" attitude in your home. Let this attitude become part of your culture of grace.

Be Nice.

> A new commandment I give to you, that you love one another:
> just as I have loved you, you also are to love one another. By this all
> people will know that you are My disciples, if you have love for one
> another. John 13:34–35

I just came from a talent show dance with my two daughters. One knew the dance well, but she was too nervous to smile. The other didn't know the dance as well, but she grinned like she was a Rockette. Guess which one the other moms complimented as a "natural dancer"?

The smile makes all the difference. I don't think my daughter felt particularly confident or happy to be on stage. But her smile made her dancing look that much more fun.

This works in families too. You can show so much grace and love by smiling. Consider this, you are living face-to-face with your family for the rest of your days. You can rearrange your face to smile and show these people that you're happy to be with them.

Smile. Hug. Offer to bring the Jell-O this year. Send birthday cards. Ask everyone how they're feeling. Tell the mamas how cute their babies are. Like their Facebook posts.

How much did all that cost you? Nothing. Maybe seventy cents for the

Jell-O. And, ahhhhh, you have brought so much joy to so many people you love. You have brought so many smiles to those who love those people. This is grace exponentially. This is a *culture* of grace.

Walk with Gratitude.

> We ought always to give thanks to God for you, brothers, as is right, because your faith is growing abundantly, and the love of every one of you for one another is increasing.   2 Thessalonians 1:3

As a chronic over-analyzer, my thoughts often feel like a merry-go-round of worry and disdain and critiquing and hope and then back to worry again. Left to my own neurotic mind, my prayers are like a ping-pong game of doubt and anxiety—far from the faith and praise I would like.

But at some point, the Holy Spirit always spritzes me with the truth of this verse: "Give thanks in all circumstances" (1 Thessalonians 5:18). Often this is the nudge I need to remember that I'm living a life designed by my Father in heaven. A good life, full of specific blessings, especially for me.

Maybe remembering this can help you too—especially when your thoughts have become a tornado of disgust for everyone around you. Or, worse, disgust for yourself.

Write down the one statement that you need God to help you with:_____. (I want to forgive my dad for his snide criticism. I need to decide if we should go on this trip. I want to hold my temper when my kids argue. I want the word "sorry" to flow off my lips a little more easily.)

Scrawl down that prayer request. Then leave the note on the counter and go for an intentional walk outside. Don't think or analyze or hold pretend debates in your brain.

Instead, notice everything: the trees, the grass, the color of the acorns against the grey dirt, the neighbor who brought your trash can in, the stoic white bird watching you, Friday, these two feet. This tree. Your family. God's care.

Then, when you walk back inside, glance at that piece of paper. More often than not, the difficult business is done. The question is easily answered and the work of forgiveness has already happened in your heart and in your mind.

And if not, then perhaps God is telling you to wait.

This is the whimsical, hard, mystical, wonderful work of the Holy Spirit.

And it works every time.

Don't Idolize. Don't Demonize.

> Blessed is the man who trusts in the LORD, whose trust is the LORD.
> Jeremiah 17:7

Because of the significant roles family members play in your life, it's so easy for your human heart to feel like it's found a savior. This is the person who is closest to you, who takes care of you in the most significant ways, who loves you in the very sweetest moments. This is the kind of love that can feel like it defines you.

Moms do this with their daughters. Grandsons with their grandfathers. Younger sisters with their older brothers. And, most certainly, wives with their husbands.

But what happens when that person lets you down? Grandpa casually says something hurtful to you. Or your daughter leaves for college, and you feel her void every minute of the day. Or your favorite uncle gets a divorce, and his world collapses and then so does his faith.

In most cases, a letdown like this can affect how we see God too. Which, of course, isn't fair at all. Because God is always God and always good and perfect. And people are always people, always changing and leaving and insulting and not seeing you as you really are and giving you bad advice and hoping you will act just like they need you to act.

For many people, the family fight they're struggling with the most is not one that started with, "He and I never got along," but more like, "She was so important to me. Then she let me down. I can't forgive her for that."

This is the lesson in all of our relationships: don't turn good things into god things. Be grateful for your family relationships because these people are good company; they make you laugh and show up when you need help. They are your people on earth, and they are all gifts from God.

But your true identity, your value, rests in His love for you. This is the love that God gives us freely in Christ and the love we all need so desperately. This is what heals your soul and shows you that it's God who is taking radical care of you. Even if the darkest days come, He has already won the battle against true evil. This same power and love lives inside of you.

Trust that *this* is the love your soul is missing. Spend time with your Lord every day and soak in His love. Know that it's this love that gives you your value.

Talk about Family Like They Are in the Room.

> So whatever you wish that others would do to you, do also to them, for this is the Law and the Prophets.   Matthew 7:12

Perhaps one of the most important habits you can practice as you cultivate a culture of grace is to watch your tongue—especially when you're talking about the struggles of another family member.

Family is a strange brew of hurt feelings, close relationships, interdependence, and the gravity of your love for one another. This concoction means you are often trying to understand someone's motivations or persuading her to do what you want. Or you're feeling hurt by her and trying to guess what he'll do next.

In short, you are probably talking about each other a lot.

Say what you have to say about other family members, but say it with tenderness. Say it as if this same family member is sitting next to you, listening to your words about her. Say it as if your words about her could change your family's entire culture.

Because they totally do.

Think about the Parable of the Lost Sheep. It matters how the shepherd treated the one wayward sheep. Imagine if he would have rolled His eyes and told the ninety-nine good sheep, "Wow. Your sister is a mess. She does the stupidest things. She has always heard her own drummer. And now I have to go look for her!" Instead of seeing the shepherd's sacrifice, the others would have listened to His words. The critical lesson about the situation would have been that this one sheep was a pain that slowed down the whole herd.

But that wasn't Jesus' message when He told the Parable of the Lost Sheep. His lesson was so much better: God loves each of us equally. He cares for each of us perfectly. God takes care of every single person because His love is all-encompassing. In His parable, Jesus doesn't make an example of the lost sheep, He teaches about the gracious shepherd.

But when we gossip about another family member, we do quite the opposite of Jesus' message. We shame the family member, instead of building the culture of grace. Think back to a time when a family member has unleashed a tirade about someone else in your herd. You know that this is not out of love. Logic—or maybe the Holy Spirit—whispers that this could easily be you on the chopping block, having everyone list your worst faults.

Change this part of your family culture. When you're talking about another family member, know that you're talking about all the family members who are listening. You're telling all of them their value. And you want them to realize that because they are your family—because they are God's children—they are valuable to you.

Celebrate Problems as Vaccinations.

> Above all, keep loving one another earnestly, since love covers a multitude of sins.
>
> 1 Peter 4:8

Infections in relationships—the problems that can spread to the whole family tree—often prompt you to search for a vaccine. Just like in the medical world, the vaccine includes a bit of the virus in it too.

For example, in our family we have a quick-tempered member. He will often yell at kids who aren't using good table manners. If you're late, he'll let you know what he thinks of that. For the rest of us, who are pretty passive about problems, his short temper stings.

Although his snapping feels like a bite from a beloved pet, when he barks at the rest of us, he often does speak the truth, and that gives us the opportunity to say, "Let's talk about this!"

This is a bit of the virus inside the vaccine. This one person's anger brings out strong feelings in us all, and we have been able to get to the heart of bigger issues because of this. Over and over, we've found ourselves hurt, then angry, then able to quickly prune the infection from the tree.

When you're struggling with a vaccine for your family's viruses, ask God what wisdom He might already be giving you. Is there a part of the virus that could be part of the vaccine? Is there a solution in the problem?

If the virus is that one person in your family feels excluded, the vaccine might be to spend more time together as a group. Maybe you have been neglecting quality time together and this bit of virus led to the vaccine. If the virus is that your brother has stopped coming to family functions, the vaccine might be that your roles and activities are outdated.

Isn't this the way grace works? The problem might be a spur to find the solution your family needed the whole time.

Sing Praises Together.

> I will sing to the LORD as long as I live;
> I will sing praise to my God while I have being.
>
> Psalm 104:33

Perhaps we are at our most exhilarated, and our most vulnerable, when we gather together to sing praises to the Lord. Among the shy tones of God's people, there is openness—a twinge of weakness and exposure.

Voices gathered together in hymns sound like hope, like joy, like strong, sure promises from our Father. This sweetness is like an injection of grace into your family, like a steroid shot to connect them quickly and in the name of the Lord.

So don't be shy, try it. Sing the Common Doxology around the hospital bed of Nana taking her last breaths—or as the newest member of your family takes some of his first breaths. Sing "Hallelujah" over and over to whatever tune you like. Sing "Jesus Loves Me" or "How Great Thou Art" or "Amazing Grace." Sing the songs the youngest kids are learning in Sunday School—the one about the hippopotamus or about Noah and the arky-arky.

Listen to the sound of your voices mingling together and forming chords you haven't heard before. And, then, emboldened by this beautiful sound, look around at the faces of your family and smile at them.

Wink at the littlest of the kids. Grin and thank the Lord for the new olive branches growing around the little circle of your family choir.

SIX.

A Tree Looks Different from Every Angle.
Change Your Perspective about Your Family!
The Difference Between Not Dying and Fully Living.

The LORD is near to all who call on Him, to all who call on Him in truth.

Psalm 145:18

After your family has survived a bitter war and come back together, everything can feel very tender and slippery. You return to one another after the screaming match of last Memorial Day, and all the branches are frozen in fear and good manners. Maybe your family tree has not died, but it's also not fully living. It's not thriving. No olive branches are growing here.

Our family has been through this, and do you know what it felt like? It felt like God had given us a delicious feast of grace, but all of us had lost our teeth. We'd forgiven, but we'd forgotten how to enjoy one another.

Trying to find your teeth again, standing in an empty kitchen with the family member who yelled, "You are not a good person!" can be just enough to make you want to join a monastery and claim you never had a family.

But God is in the awkwardness. He's in the silences. He is in those first self-conscious hugs. He's there because He is the one who gives you a new heart, a soul that His grace has tenderized.

Be patient here, but also be proactive. Your family is in a vulnerable spot right now, like refugees from a war zone. Welcome them into the culture of grace by applying some of the lessons you learned from the conflict.

Be careful about touchy subjects. Give extra care to those black sheep who have been away from the family. Show them that this is a family where grace lives.

Try to See Your Family Members as Who They Are Now.

There shall come forth a shoot from the stump of Jesse,

> and a branch from his roots shall bear fruit.
> And the Spirit of the LORD shall rest upon him,
>   the Spirit of wisdom and understanding,
>   the Spirit of counsel and might,
>   the Spirit of knowledge and the fear of the LORD.
>
> Isaiah 11:1–2

Life changes at a constant and aggressive pace. Every second of every minute, our bodies and souls and relationships and interests and outlook are evolving and adjusting.

Your body is changing constantly. My cousin was allergic to peanuts and now he's not. My friend (from an island) loves shellfish, but the food now makes her break out in hives.

Yet we all seem to believe that our souls cannot change. Not really. Yes, you believe the one about my friend not getting to eat shrimp, but if I tell you that my cousin stole all our money and then repented, you might advise me not to trust him again.

What is this? Our bodies are elastic, but our souls are not? That doesn't make sense. Especially not for us as Christians. Because the whole point of God is that He makes things new and different. Remember, total destruction . . . and then an olive branch? The same power that created that miracle is creating a miracle inside each of us. The same knitting that's healing the cut on my finger is threading together new faith in my soul.

You either believe that God can make you a new creation, that you will be totally transformed by the work of the Holy Spirit, and that other people can be completely changed by the miracle of forgiveness . . . or you don't.

If you want a family tree of olive branches—a culture of grace in your family—then believe in this kind of radical transformation. Believe that anything can happen. Believe that God can change anyone. Believe that your uncle you knew last decade might be different now. In his place is a gentler, more patient new creation.

And, yes, believe that you can forgive. Absolutely yes—love wins and grace comes through. If it hasn't, maybe it's not the end of the story.

Hallelujah and praise the Lord!

The Aunties and the Uncles.

> If you then, who are evil, know how to give good gifts to your children, how much more will the heavenly Father give the Holy Spirit to those who ask Him! Luke 11:13

Give your kids the gift of a chance to spend time with the other branches in your family tree, especially with their aunts and uncles, your brothers and sisters.

In the intertwined web of relationships and family, these men and women can become the best advice-givers, the gift-givers, the zoo chaperones, and the prayer partners that are missing in your kids' lives.

Maybe you still see your siblings exactly as they've always been (bossy, stingy, controlling, angry, or irresponsible). But your kids, the next generation, might not see them like that at all. In fact, your kids will see your brothers and sisters completely differently than you do.

This is one of those special miracles of family: what you've always seen as your sister's laziness, your kids might appreciate as patience. You really can't stand fishing, but your brother offers to take your son. You've never understood your sister's preoccupation with disassembling every electronic. But now your daughter is the same way, and they can talk about how cell phones work together.

What a strange, wonderful blessing of family.

God's work is brilliant. Celebrate it and send your kids off to their aunt's house for a few hours.

When One Family Member Pushes Your Buttons.

> Let the one who is taught the word share all good things with the one who teaches. Do not be deceived: God is not mocked, for whatever one sows, that will he also reap. For the one who sows to his own flesh will from the flesh reap corruption, but the one who sows to the Spirit will from the Spirit reap eternal life. Galatians 6:6–8

When there's one family member who lies to you, finds your faults, doesn't seem to like you, ask God to change your perspective from victim to helper.

Try to find something about this person you admire, like, or respect. (Everyone has something.) Remind yourself of this before, during, and after you encounter this person. Ask God to help you remember that relationships are actually mirrors—the way you treat your uncle who is on the far opposite of the political spectrum is usually the same way he'll treat you in return.

And, of course, keep coming to this person's worth as a member of your family. Remember that God tells us to love our neighbors—the ones closest to us—and like it or not, this person is your neighbor.

Take Not Your Holy Spirit from Me.

> But the Helper, the Holy Spirit, whom the Father will send in My name, He will teach you all things and bring to your remembrance all that I have said to you. John 14:26

The Holy Spirit seems to do the best work with me when I'm in the shower. This is when I get away from the distractions of my buzzing mind and listen to the quiet part of my heart. This is also when I become aware of all the anger and bitterness I'm holding on to. These are the two emotions that bubble up first, and they also point to the deeper wounds that need healing. These wounds need God because these are the two emotions that bubble up first.

In the quiet of the shower, away from my vibrating phone, I can hear the Holy Spirit whispering that God loves me and that He takes care of me as tenderly as a parent cares for a sick child. The Spirit helps me to forgive, opens my eyes to ways I can better love, softens my heart to be more tender.

What is your shower, the time and place where the Holy Spirit comes in and moves around the deep hurts in your soul? Maybe it's kneeling during your early-morning prayer time? Perhaps as you're falling asleep at night? When you receive Communion? When a friend encourages you? When you hear God's Word?

This place, these realizations, this healing, all this changing and opening and rearranging is the work of your heavenly Father, who loves you.

And it is a blessing, given to us through the blood of Jesus Christ.

Everywhere you are.

What Culture Are You Building?

> So, every healthy tree bears good fruit, but the diseased tree bears bad fruit. A healthy tree cannot bear bad fruit, nor can a diseased tree bear good fruit. Every tree that does not bear good fruit is cut down and thrown into the fire.　　　　　Matthew 7:17–19

So many parents I interviewed had such high expectations for their kids and their future relationships. The parents said, "We want our family to be highly functioning." "I hope my boys are so close, they don't even have to call each other on holidays because they're already at each other's house." "My greatest hope, more than anything else, is that my kids know for sure that their family is the one that takes care of them."

But the crazy part is that all of these same people are struggling to get along with their own adult siblings. We have sky-high expectations for what we will do with the next generation, but we don't realize that what we're doing right now, with our very own brothers and sisters, is what will actually determine that. You are building a culture with the next generation by how you're treating this generation.

So try this. Write down three words that describe your culture in your childhood home. Now write down three that describe the culture in your home today. What's similar? What are you doing better? What can you improve?

Now, write a prayer asking God to provide The Next Right Thing, the next good intention, the love, the grace, the next olive branch. Ask Him to change your culture so it glorifies Him.

Practice Patience with Tough Family Situations.

> And we know that for those who love God all things work together for good, for those who are called according to His purpose.
> 　　　　　Romans 8:28

When it comes to families, we really want neat, linear, efficient solutions. We want God to be on call like a particularly doting customer service rep. We don't want to think about how He allowed generations to wander in the wilderness for years. Yuck. We would prefer to learn lessons from Facebook status updates or through one funny and light conversation with an excellent conversationalist.

This is the truth I've discovered as I've grown older: the very sweetest parts of life will take lots of time to unfold. And the lessons we learn from waiting patiently for His timing, from trusting God for provision, from living as His children of faith are among the most important we can understand this side of heaven.

The lesson of patience—this very sweet fruit of the Spirit—is the one that can help you through so much of life, so many other struggles. God might teach it to you through your family, but it will serve you through every other part of your life as well.

SEVEN.

Fertilize the Seeds of Faith and Root Your Family in the Holy Ground of God's Word and Love. Study the Bible Together!

Letters to Jesus.

> Peace I leave with you; My peace I give to you. Not as the world gives do I give to you. Let not your hearts be troubled, neither let them be afraid.　　　　　　　　　　　　　　　　John 14:27

Letter writing can be a powerful form of prayer. Sometimes, when you're not sure what your family needs, writing a letter directly to Jesus opens up your thoughts, concerns, deepest desires, gratitude, and praise. Addressing your pen-and-paper letter to your Savior (the very One who went to the cross for you and who takes care of your greatest needs . . . and tiniest needs) can feel so comforting.

Knowing and trusting the power of His love and mercy can help you to overcome the fear to articulate the change you hope to see in your family.

So what will you ask Jesus to do? Will the transformation in your family be a conversation? a big family meal where everyone can come together to talk face-to-face? better daily communication? a deeper commitment? less isolation from one another?

Start your letter, "Dear Jesus . . ." and write that right now.

Worship Together.

> Addressing one another in psalms and hymns and spiritual songs,
> singing and making melody to the LORD with your heart.
>
> Ephesians 5:19

Maybe your family meets often for worship. Yours is one of those multi-generational clans that fills several pews at the church. Maybe this is the same church that your grandpa helped build and where your kids still go to Vacation Bible School. Maybe you know the joy of hearing your mom's voice harmonize with your daughter's voice in a gorgeous family tree duet.

Or maybe your situation is more typical. Your family is flung far from one another, and you rarely ever kneel together for Confession or raise your hands in praise together.

Or maybe your worship history is filled with so many disappointments and hurts that you can more likely imagine kneeling next to Lady Gaga than you can imagine receiving Communion next to your own parents.

But you probably have had the experience of worshiping with your family at a Baptism or Christmas Eve services or an Easter sunrise service. Whatever the occasion—once in a lifetime or once a week—you've surely felt the deep joy that comes from worshiping with those who know you best.

Worshiping with your family is about so much more than what's happening in your little pew. It's a foretaste of heaven. It's a glimpse of how it will feel for us to be united with all the angels and archangels and the whole company of heaven.

It's about coming to the table together and eating the Body of Christ and drinking the blood of our Savior. It's about hearing the Word and collectively letting those seeds of faith find root in our individual souls. It's gathering the hands of all the generations in prayer and petition. Separate, yes, but very much together.

Find a way to gather your family at church. Or, when you're together and far from a church, worship around Granny's hospital bed or the campfire at the annual family reunion.

Coming together in mutual adoration and humbleness, before the Lord who has stitched you all together, is the tiny bud of an olive branch.

Planting the Next Generation.

> You shall therefore lay up these words of mine in your heart and in your soul, and you shall bind them as a sign on your hand, and they shall be as frontlets between your eyes. You shall teach them to your children, talking of them when you are sitting in your house, and when you are walking by the way, and when you lie down, and when you rise. You shall write them on the doorposts of your house and on your gates, that your days and the days of your children may be multiplied in the land that the LORD swore to your fathers to give them, as long as the heavens are above the earth.
>
> Deuteronomy 11:18–21

The most important nutrient you can give your family tree is God's Word. Pass it down to your kids through devotions, worship, and in your conversations. Share it with your parents and your brothers and sisters and your aunts and uncles. Spread the Word of God because we know that there is power in His Word. We trust that the Word of God doesn't return empty (see Isaiah 55:11). Faith comes to those who hear (see Romans 10:17), and faith is the seed of what grows into a culture of grace.

Create opportunities to share the Word of God with your family. Write your favorite Bible verses in your kids' Bibles. Assign a special verse to each child and repeat it to them often. My parents give each of our kids a verse for the year, and they find opportunities to talk to each child about their special verse.

When you pray before the hot dogs on Labor Day, pray Ephesians 4:2, asking God to bless your family with humbleness and patience. Create a family blessing from Romans 15:13 ("May the God of hope fill you with all joy and peace in believing, so that by the power of the Holy Spirit you may abound in hope"), and speak that blessing over one another when you leave the family reunion, when you gather on Good Friday, and before you tear the wrapping paper off Christmas gifts.

More Than Just a Donor Match.

> By this we know love, that He laid down His life for us, and we ought to lay down our lives for the brothers. But if anyone has the world's goods and sees his brother in need, yet closes his heart against him, how does God's love abide in him? Little children, let us not love in word or talk but in deed and in truth. By this we shall know that we

> are of the truth and reassure our heart before Him; for whenever our
> heart condemns us, God is greater than our heart, and He knows
> everything.   1 John 3:16–20

Parents often prompt their kids to get along with one another. But why? Perhaps it's this. Your mom and dad understand they will most likely die before you do. When you can't call your parents for advice, you will need someone else you can turn to. If you're connected to your siblings, you can lean on them for help and advice.

This is a very good reason to plant the roots of your family tree in the Word of God. The habits and relationships you're encouraging in them right now will be the habits and relationships that see them through the hardest times of their lives.

By sharing the Word of God with your family, you're helping them feel comfortable with talking about Jesus and forgiveness. When you pray together as a group, you're teaching them how to pray. You're digging the intentional tunnels for these dear people to connect on a deeper, spiritual level. You're giving them the maps to one another, so they can find one another if you're not there one day.

Habits stick. In a culture of grace, you can teach your family members the values and practices that will define who they are—children of God.

You (Yes, YOU!) Can Be the Transformative Generation.

> Do not be conformed to this world, but be transformed by the renewal of your mind, that by testing you may discern what is the will of God, what is good and acceptable and perfect.
>   Romans 12:2

Perhaps the hardest part of changing your family's culture is to learn to trust God. It's especially hard to trust that God can transform your heart, that He can transform your family.

The idea of this can feel impossible—especially if your family is coming out of a really tough past. Your future might look predetermined, like you have to follow the same cycles of your parents, like God is a copy machine assigning the same struggles and curses to every generation.

But He isn't. Maybe that's what the world wants us to believe, but God tells us to not be conformed to this world. He tells us that His will is good and acceptable and perfect.

So, what would this transformation look like in your family? What sanctification and work can happen in your lifetime, so you can pass down a better grace-filled life to the next generation? How can He change you through His Word, through His love, so you are different?

Write these thoughts out in a prayer. Trust that God can make you the transformative generation between a culture of brokenness and a culture of grace.

Training Wheels for Life.

> I will not leave you as orphans; I will come to you.
>
> John 14:18

Anyone who has taught a kid to ride a bike knows the importance of training wheels. They are the first step toward the big pay-off, toward the radical independence your child needs, so he can to cruise down the sidewalk without you holding on.

Thanks to the crutch of training wheels, the kid gets the feel of balancing. He learns to trust himself. To feel the exhilaration of the breeze and the thrill of traveling faster than he can run.

This seems to be God's plan for birthing us into families, to teach us how to do relationships within the safe confines of our own first clan. With this first group, you learn all the exhilaration of joy and love. You learn how to laugh together and how to celebrate one another and how to fight. It's in your family that you first learn to trust and love and support and care for others.

After these first tiny relationships bloom, you start to understand how to love the rest of the world. You understand forgiveness for your ex-husband by the grace your sister showed you when you broke her roller skates. You understand the fun of meeting friends for dinner by the silly suppers you used to have with your family.

This is the soil for your family's future. Teach them the right lessons. Teach them the culture of grace by showing them who God is, by living His love out in the most intentional ways. You understand the constant care that relationships need by the notes your mom put in your lunch box every day.

And then pray that they will teach the world these same lessons.

Your Family as It Is in Heaven.

> So Mephibosheth lived in Jerusalem, for he ate always at the king's table. Now he was lame in both his feet.
>
> 2 Samuel 9:13

Living in a culture of grace is actually your life here on earth as it is in heaven. Your identity as a child of God is your identity in heaven—and it's who you truly are on earth too. Living as a child of God becomes the identity through which you see the rest of the world.

In conclusion, it's critically important for you to understand the significance of your heavenly Father adopting you to be one of His own children. He makes you who you are. And by His love, you are empowered to love your family—*on earth as it is in heaven.*

In 2 Samuel is the story of a lame man, Mephibosheth, whom King David adopts to be his own. This lame orphan becomes the son of the actual king. When David adopts his friend Jonathan's son (who is also the grandson of his enemy Saul), he gives him lots of land and riches. Most important, King David invites Mephibosheth to eat dinner with him every night. He gives him the kind of infinite love that this rejected, crippled man must have been searching for his whole life.

This is the kind of infinite grace and love that God gives you too. And it's the kind He commands you to show your family—those nearest to your heart—these very close relationships that God has assigned to you.

What does this really mean—except that it means everything? This means that the way you treat your flesh-and-blood family is absolutely different forever because of God's love for you in Christ Jesus, because of your adoption and His care for you.

Amen.

Acknowledgements

Thank you to my family: first, to my husband, Mike, the love of my life. You have taught me that family is the most important thing—next to God's love. Thank you for walking beside me every step as we raise our kids in a culture of grace.

And to our four kids: Catie, for writing me sweet notes and always encouraging me. Sam, for praying over me so many times. Elisabeth, for modeling true passion to spread God's Word. Nate, for rolling with our busy household with such a happy heart.

To my mom and dad, Ken and Virginia Buehring, for teaching me what grace looks like, and for moving closer to us so we can do life together.

Mark and Marcilee, you are examples of grace, generosity, and love. Thanks for being in-laws who shine God's grace to all the generations of your family tree.

To everyone at Concordia Publishing House: Peggy Kuethe, through more than a decade of books and projects, you have been the very best editor. Thank you for your faithfulness, your keen eye, your encouragement, and your enthusiasm for this project. You are gifted and such a gift.

Elizabeth and Lindsey, you are both so creative, so bright, and so helpful. I'm blessed to work with you both every day.

Holli and the other marketing team, thanks for all the work on the cover.

To my dear friends: Amanda Gatton, you amaze me with your creativity and servant heart. Your abilities to organize, write postcards, create beautiful gifts, speed text, and show up are gifts from God.

Melissa and Scott, Connie and Sean, Jen and Kenny, Rosemary, Barb, Janet, Joy, Amy, Mrs. Judy, April, Katie and Fred, Christine, Hannah and Laura, Kay, and Bonnie, thanks for talking with me about family and grace and for sharing your stories and insights. Also, thanks for opening your home to our kids and encouraging me. You are our family's village and we love you.

Our Launch Team—you are a wonderful group of servant hearts, willing to spread hope for the future generations. Thank you.

Most of all, to our heavenly Father. Isn't His design of families just breathtaking in its genius? Brilliant and so, so loving.